Cybersecurity – A Broad Perspective

Cybersecurity – A Broad Perspective

Dr. Ambika Nagaraj

CWP

For more information about the books published by Central West Publishing PTY LTD, please visit https://centralwestpublishing.com

Disclaimer
Every effort has been made by the publisher, editors and authors while preparing this book, however, no warranties are made regarding the accuracy and completeness of the content. The publisher, editors and authors disclaim without any limitation all warranties as well as any implied warranties about sales, along with fitness of the content for a particular purpose. Citation of any website and other information sources does not mean any endorsement from the publisher, editors and authors. For ascertaining the suitability of the contents contained herein for a particular lab or commercial use, consultation with the subject expert is needed. In addition, while using the information and methods contained herein, the practitioners and researchers need to be mindful for their own safety, along with the safety of others, including the professional parties and premises for whom they have professional responsibility. To the fullest extent of law, the publisher, editors and authors are not liable in all circumstances (special, incidental, and consequential) for any injury and/or damage to persons and property, along with any potential loss of profit and other commercial damages due to the use of any methods, products, guidelines, procedures contained in the material herein.

NATIONAL LIBRARY OF AUSTRALIA

A catalogue record for this book is available from the National Library of Australia

ISBN (print): 978-1-922617-74-3

Foreword

Welcome to the enormous realm of cybersecurity, where endless possibilities and hidden vulnerabilities are woven into the very fabric of our digital existence. In "Cybersecurity: A Broad Perspective," we take an expedition that goes beyond data security and explores the essence of our digital connectivity, demonstrating how crucial it is to defend our cybersecurity environment.

The book sets the stage, painting a vivid portrait of the intricate relationship between our lives and technology. Even as we relish the many opportunities presented by networked systems, we cannot overlook the looming threat of previously unseen difficulties that require our prompt attention and action. This book serves as a sentinel, a defender of the faith that people have in our digital infrastructure, and a helper as they navigate the challenges associated with cybersecurity. The narrative within these pages isn't designed to instill fear but to empower. It gives us the essential knowledge needed to safely traverse the digital sphere. Understanding the nature of cyber threats , the methods wielded by malicious actors , and the defence strategies available strengthens our arsenal in fortifying our digital defense.

Cybersecurity is the foundation of economies, the guardian of individual privacy, and the barrier to vital services; it is not an add-on. Cyberthreats are a real threat to everyone, including individuals, global organizations, financial institutions, and healthcare systems. As such, we must all work together with unflinching resolve to strengthen our defenses. The book isn't just a dossier of threats posed by cyberattacks; it's a roadmap to detection methodologies and preventive measures. It's a call to action for continual learning , adaptability, and the shared responsibility to protect our digital commons

Let's face the seriousness of the obstacles ahead and acknowledge the chances for collaboration, creativity, and fortitude that lurk in the shadow of adversity as we traverse this terrain. When we work together, we have the ability to create a digital environment that is not only highly capable but also steadfastly secure. When we collaborate , we can build a digital environment that is unwaveringly safe while remaining immensely powerful

Aryan Chaudhary
Chief Scientific Advisor, Biotech Sphere Research, India
Chair, Meerut ACM Professional Chapter

■■

In the dynamic landscape of our digital era, where the intricate threads of our lives are interwoven with technology, the significance of cybersecurity cannot be emphasized enough. As we embrace the limitless potential of interconnected systems, we are met with unprecedented challenges that require our unwavering attention, understanding, and proactive measures.

This preface serves as a portal into the realm of cybersecurity, a discipline that extends far beyond the mere protection of data. It stands as a vigilant guardian, preserving the trust in the digital infrastructure that shapes our daily existence. With our increasing reliance on smart devices, cloud computing, and interconnected networks, the vulnerabilities inherent in this digital frontier become more apparent.

Cybersecurity is not merely an accessory to our technological pursuits; it is an imperative that underpins the integrity of economies, the sanctity of personal privacy, and the continuity of essential services. From financial institutions to healthcare systems, individual users to multinational corporations, the specter of cyber threats looms large, necessitating a collective and unwavering commitment to fortify our digital defense.

The exploration into the cybersecurity domain embarked upon in this book is not intended to instill fear but rather to empower. By comprehending the nature of cyber threats, understanding the methodologies employed by malicious actors, and becoming familiar with the strategies available for defense, we equip ourselves with the knowledge necessary to navigate the digital landscape securely. This journey requires continual learning, adaptability, and a shared responsibility to protect the digital commons.

As we embark on this exploration, let us acknowledge the gravity of the challenges ahead and recognize the opportunities for cooperation, innovation, and resilience that arise in the face of adversity. Together, we can construct a digital world that is sophisticated in its capabilities and steadfast in its security.

This book delves into the threats posed by cyber-attacks, the methodologies to detect them, and security measures to prevent them. Welcome to the world of cybersecurity, where vigilance is the currency of trust, and knowledge is the key to resilience

Manish Thakral
Consultant, Deloitte India
Risk Advisory - Cyber: Cyber Strategy

■■

The author published many articles and books related to IoT, Algorithms, Data Science in the field of computer science. Now the author placed an extra effort to expresses cybersecurity threats, issues and different methodologies which is very useful for the society. The book focused on recent trends of cyber security which is very useful for research and industry development. The problem-solving approach author narrated effectively and in an understandable manner. The strategies used to solve the issues, algorithms related cyber security, types of treats and how to manage treats are narrated in this book.

Dr. Krishnan Rajamany
Associate Professor,
School of Mathematics & Natural Sciences,
Chanakya University, Bangalore, India

■■

In recent times, it has been keenly observed that individuals and organizations are in the trauma of complex problems when it comes to protecting their data as well as IT infrastructure. Owing to the rocket high shooting in cybercrimes, it becomes crucial to implement efficient cybersecurity protocols and strategies. The pivotal aspect is to secure data, operations, processes, software, hardware, networks, and technology at all costs. The severity arises due to innovation in hacking via advanced technologies like artificial intelligence and social engineering which aid in gaining access to systems and data. The attackers are becoming more fluent in using powerful malware, spyware, and other viruses. They can easily scan infrastructures, programs, and networks; intrigue defects, and compromise the users' accounts. The book Cybersecurity - A Broad Perspective gives a comprehensive usage of cybersecurity systems to prevent theft, damage, unauthorized access, and cyberattacks on mandate digital infrastructures. It utilizes extensive tools, procedures, and methodologies to guarantee the privacy, availability, and integrity of the cybersecurity system. This book uncovers several applications of cybersecurity and highlights the importance of securing cyberspaces. It unfurls how organizations and governments are now willing to invest more time, money, and resources to improve cybersecurity measures, decrease security risks, and prevent cyberattacks. The editors have done a commendable job at all stages and ensured that the chapters are reviewed by reputed reviewers. This book can be used as a reference book by researchers, academics, practitioners, policymakers, and postgraduate students in the areas of information technology, network security surveillance, risk management, business continuity, digital defense mechanism, and many more.

Dr. Arti Jain,
Department of Computer Science & Engineering and Information
Technology
Jaypee Institute of Information Technology,
Noida, Uttar Pradesh, India

••

In our digital world, where technology weaves into every aspect of our lives, understanding cybersecurity is more crucial than ever. This book is your guide into this essential realm. Think of cybersecurity as the guardian of trust in our digital lives. As we rely on smart devices and interconnected networks, the need to protect our digital world becomes clear. It's not just about securing data; it's about safeguarding the integrity of economies, personal privacy, and essential services.

This journey into cybersecurity isn't about scaring you but empowering you. By understanding cyber threats and how to defend against them, you gain the knowledge to navigate our digital world securely. It's an ongoing journey of learning, adaptability, and shared responsibility to protect our digital space.

As we embark on this exploration, let us grasp the gravity of the challenges ahead and recognize the opportunities for cooperation, innovation, and resilience that emerge in the face of adversity. Together, we can construct a digital world that is sophisticated in its capabilities and steadfast in its security.

This book covers the basics: threats from cyber-attacks, how to detect them, and security measures to prevent them. Welcome to the world of cybersecurity, where vigilance builds trust, and knowledge ensures resilience.

Dr. Gururaj H L
Researcher & Academician
Manipal Institute of Technology, Bengaluru

■■■

As a teacher of Computer Science and Engineering for undergraduate and postgraduate students, I have been always looking for the books with deeper insights on latest technological developments. Dr. Ambika, with her simplicity in writing has attracted my attention in her earlier books. Her vast knowledge on the subject matter and simple examples and case studies keeps reader connected and involved with the flow. Cyber security has been a buzzword in recent past with internet entering in all domains in the universe. It has been challenging for the technocrats to explain its impacts, threats and preventions to anyone in general. Dr. Ambika with her effortless style of making understand complex technical topics has come up with her this new book. I am equally excited to see people close to me, my students, coming up with a better version of their cyber security knowledge after going through this book, as do I.

Dr. Geeta Tripathi, Professor, CSE,
Guru Nanak University, Hyderabad

■■■

In an era where our very existence is intertwined with the digital realm, "Cybersecurity - A Broad Perspective", authored by Ambika Nagaraj emerges not just as a book but as an essential guide for navigating the complex and ever-evolving world of digital security. The pages within this volume offer far more than mere technical insight;

they provide a panoramic view of how cybersecurity is inextricably linked to every facet of our modern lives.

As you embark upon this enlightening journey, you will discover that cybersecurity transcends the traditional boundaries of protecting data and systems. It is a vibrant field that safeguards the trust we place in our digital infrastructure, a trust that shapes our daily interactions, our businesses, our governance, and even our personal privacy.

It serves as a beacon, guiding us through the complexities of cybersecurity with clarity and wisdom. As you delve into these pages, you will gain a deeper understanding of the nature of cyber threats, the tactics of adversaries, and, most importantly, the means by which we can defend ourselves and our communities.

In an age where cyber threats are an ever-present spectre, this book is a testament to the power of knowledge and vigilance. It invites us to appreciate the gravity of the challenges we face while recognizing the immense opportunities for cooperation, innovation, and resilience that arise in adversity.

Dr Rashmi Singh
Associate Professor, AIAS, Amity University
Co-Series Editor, Taylor & Francis

Preface

The importance of cybersecurity in the rapidly changing digital world, when technology is intricately intertwined into every aspect of our lives, cannot be understated. As we embrace the limitless potential of linked systems, we are faced with previously unheard-of difficulties that call for our consideration, comprehension, and constructive action.

This introduction provides a preamble to the terrifying field of cybersecurity, which goes well beyond data protection. It is a watchful defender of the faith in the digital infrastructure that guides our day-to-day activities. As our reliance on smart gadgets, cloud computing, and linked networks grows, so do the dangers that come with living in this digital frontier.

Cybersecurity is a need that supports the integrity of economies, the right to privacy, and the provision of basic services. It is not only nice to have for our technical endeavors. The threat of cyberattacks looms big over financial institutions, healthcare systems, individual users, and global organizations. We must all make a firm commitment to strengthening our digital defenses.

This investigation into the field of cybersecurity aims to empower rather than to frighten. Through comprehending the characteristics of cyber threats, the techniques used by malevolent entities, and the defensive tactics at our disposal, we arm ourselves with the information required to securely traverse the digital terrain. The path demands ongoing education, flexibility, and a cooperative effort to safeguard the digital commons.

As we embark on this investigation, let us acknowledge the seriousness of the tasks that lay ahead and the chances for collaboration, creativity, and fortitude that appear when faced with difficulty. By working together, we can create a digital environment that is both highly capable and firmly secure.

The book covers the risks associated with cyberattacks, how to identify them, and basic security precautions to keep them at bay. Greetings from the realm of cybersecurity, where knowledge is the key to resilience and alertness is the currency of trust.

Table of Contents

CHAPTER 1

INTRODUCTION TO CYBERSECURITY

Abstract

In today's digitally connected world, cybersecurity has become a crucial subject since it shields data, networks, and systems from a variety of cyber threats. Together with technology, malicious actors' methods for exploiting flaws and endangering the security of individuals, organizations, and governments are also evolving. The practice of stopping unauthorized access, attacks, theft, or damage to computer systems, networks, and data is known as cybersecurity. To create a secure digital workplace, processes, technology, and awareness campaigns must be implemented. Because of this, cybersecurity is a multidisciplinary approach that makes use of a range of methods, instruments, and technologies to protect the accessibility, privacy, and integrity of digital assets. This chapter summarises the many types of cybercrimes, the variables that influence them, and the necessity of cybersecurity.

Keywords: information security, cybersecurity, cybercrime

1.1 Introduction

Information security is often referred to as cybersecurity (Thakur & Pathan, 2020) (Thames & Schaefer, 2017). It involves safeguarding computer systems, networks, data, and digital assets from theft, unauthorized interruption, cyber threats, and other unauthorized access, damage, and/or loss. It entails putting policies, procedures, tools, and best practices into action to guarantee the privacy, accuracy, and accessibility of data and resources.

Minimizing the risks associated with cyber threats and ensuring that data and systems are safe from a variety of attacks, such as ransomware (Farion-Melnyk, Rozheliuk, Slipchenko, & Banakh, 2021), phishing (Qabajeh, Thabtah, & Chiclana, 2018), malware (Sudhakar & Kumar, 2020), denial of service (DoS) attacks, and more, are the main objectives of cybersecurity. Detecting, averting, responding to, and recovering from any cyber events are all part of cybersecurity activities, which aim to minimize potential harm and protect the digital ecosystem. Figure 1.1 represents Cybersecurity paradigms.

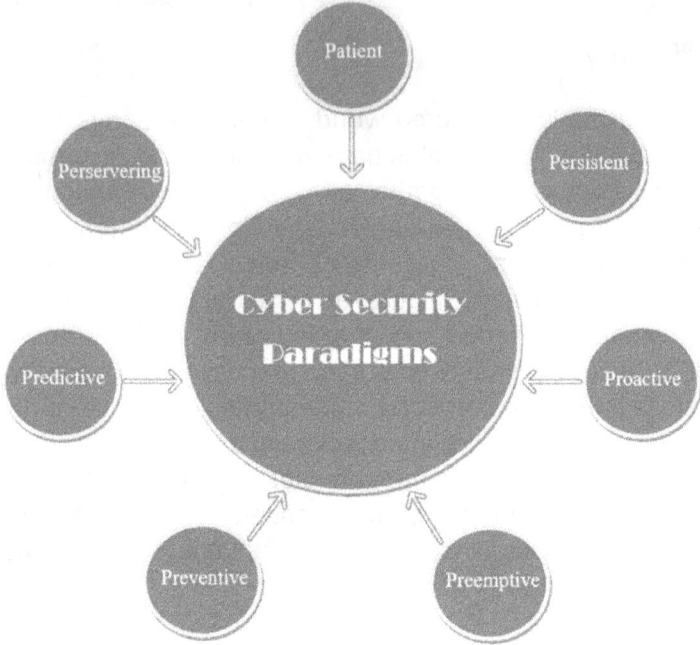

Figure 1.1 Cybersecurity paradigms (Safitra, Lubis, & Fakhrurroja, 2023).

1.2 History and Analysis of Internet

The progression of technology, communication, and societal transformation is intricate and intriguing, as evidenced by the history and study of the cyber world. This section will give a brief synopsis of the major turning points and advancements in the history of cyberspace, and then analyze its effects on the economy, society, and culture.

- **Origins (1960s-1970s):** The ARPANET project, run by the US Department of Defence, began in the 1960s to develop a decentralized communication network that would be resistant to nuclear assaults. The Transmission Control Protocol (TCP) and Internet Protocol (IP) suite, which are the

2

cornerstones of the contemporary cyber world, were created by ARPANET.

- **Expanding Network (1980s):** As universities, research centers, and commercial organizations started joining the network, the Internet began to grow beyond its military roots in the 1980s. When the Domain Name System (DNS) was first implemented in 1983, numerical IP addresses could be linked to human-readable domain names.
- **World Wide Web (1990s):** In 1989, British computer scientist Tim Berners-Lee created the World Wide Web and used a graphical user interface and hypertext to make it available to a wider audience. When the first web browser was introduced in 1990, information sharing and access were completely transformed.
- **Commercialization and Growth (late 1990s-early 2000s):** The commercialization and use of the Internet both increased significantly in the 1990s. The internet became a vital resource for both personal and professional usage with the introduction of web-based email, e-commerce platforms, and search engines like Google.
- **Social Media and Web 2.0 (mid-2000s):** The emergence of social media platforms such as Facebook (Van Dijck, 2013) (Wilson, Gosling, & Graham, 2012), YouTube (Orús, et al., 2016), and Twitter (Murthy, 2018) in the mid-2000s enabled user-generated content and interaction. The emphasis of this era—often referred to as Web 2.0—was on participation, cooperation, and information exchange.
- **Mobile and Connectivity (late 2000s-2010s):** Mobile internet usage increased dramatically in the late 2000s as a result of the widespread use of smartphones and other mobile devices. People may now access information and services while they're on the road because of its increased accessibility and ubiquity.
- **IoT and Future Trends (2010s-present):** With the emergence of the Internet of Things (IoT), data gathering and automation became possible by linking items and devices to the Internet. The internet will change in the future due to emerging technologies like edge computing, blockchain, 5G, and

artificial intelligence (AI), which promise faster, more secure, and more efficient connections.

Analysis of the Internet's Impact:

- **Global Communication and Information Access:** Because it allows for real-time worldwide exchanges, the internet has completely changed communication. It's a major tool for gathering data, carrying out research, and keeping up with current affairs, which has an impact on research, journalism, and education.
- **Economic Transformation:** New markets, possibilities, and business models have been generated by it. The economy is significantly impacted by digital advertising, e-commerce, internet banking, and remote labor. It has also made it possible for people to create internet enterprises with little initial investment, which is known as entrepreneurship.
- **Social and Cultural Changes:** The way individuals connect, engage, and exchange experiences has been completely transformed by social media and online communities. It has affected society's views, actions, and cultural trends. It brought up issues with internet harassment, false information, and privacy.
- **Cybersecurity and Privacy Concerns:** The interconnectedness of technology has given rise to serious worries about data leaks, privacy, and cybersecurity. It is now extremely difficult to protect sensitive and personal data, which calls for stronger cybersecurity regulations and laws.
- **Education and Learning:** With the availability of digital libraries, educational materials, and online courses, it has completely changed the way people learn. It has made education more flexible and accessible by promoting lifetime learning and skill development.
- **Political and Civic Engagement:** Political procedures have been affected, making way for internet activism, campaigns, and greater public participation. It has altered how citizens engage in democratic processes and obtain political information.

4

- **Challenges and Inequalities:** Disparities in internet access contribute to the digital divide, which is still a major problem, especially in underprivileged areas and communities. To guarantee equitable opportunities and access to information, it is imperative to address these gaps.

1.3 What is Cybercrime?

Cybercrime is the term for illegal actions committed online, mainly using computers, networks, and the internet. These illegal activities frequently aim to hurt, destabilize, or create financial loss by targeting specific people, groups, governments, or whole countries. Cybercrime is a broad category of criminal activity that changes as technology develops and criminals discover new methods to take advantage of weaknesses.

Cybercrime is a serious threat to people, companies, and governments. It can result in money losses, privacy violations, harm to one's reputation, and even legal repercussions. Strong cybersecurity measures, public awareness campaigns, laws, international collaboration, and continuous improvements in security protocols and technology are all necessary components of a multipronged strategy to combat cybercrime.

1.4 History of cybercrime

Cybercrime's origins may be traced to the early years of computer technology when networks and computers were first used for evil purposes. This is a list of significant dates in the history of cybercrime, organized chronologically:

- **1960s and 1970s: The Birth of Computer Intrusions** - The 1960s and 1970s saw the earliest occurrences of system intrusion and unauthorized access. One well-known example is the early 1960s invention of the game "Spacewar!" by MIT student Steve Russell. To play the game without permission, people started breaking into the system.
- **1980s: The Era of Hacking and Malware** - Malicious software creation and hacking witnessed a sharp increase in the

1980s. The phrase "computer virus" was first used in 1983 by computer scientist Fred Cohen, who also created a self-replicating program to prove its existence. Prominent malware, such as the Morris Worm from 1988, demonstrated the possibility of major disruptions brought on by unapproved software.

- **1990s: The Rise of Cybercrime and Commercial Exploitation** - Cybercrime increased significantly in the 1990s. Cybercriminals started making money off of the internet. In 1988, the "Morris Worm," the first large cyberattack, propagated over the early internet and caused severe disruptions. Hacking teams such as Lizard Squad and hacker Kevin Mitnick were well-known for their exploits in the mid-1990s.

- **Late 1990s and Early 2000s: The Dot-Com Bubble and Pioneering Attacks** - The internet's exponential growth during the dot-com boom attracted hackers. The "ILOVEYOU" worm, which caused extensive damage in 2000, and the Code Red and Nimda worms, which affected millions of computers in 2001, are two notable assaults that occurred during this time.

- **Mid-2000s: The Rise of Phishing and Identity Theft** - Phishing attacks, in which fraudsters deceive users into divulging personal information like passwords and credit card numbers, increased dramatically in the mid-2000s. Data breaches and identity theft increased in frequency, affecting both people and businesses.

- **Late 2000s: Advanced Persistent Threats (APTs) and Ransomware** - In the late 2000s, nation-states were frequently implicated in sophisticated, protracted cyber espionage efforts known as Advanced Persistent Threats (APTs). Ransomware also became a cyber menace around this time, encrypting files and requesting a fee to unlock them.

- **2010s and Beyond: Increased Sophistication and Diversification of Cyber Threats** - The decade of the 2010s witnessed a sharp rise in the sophistication of cybercrime, with nation-states waging wars and conducting cyber espionage. High-profile breaches, like the Equifax hack in 2017 and the Target breach in 2013, exposed the personal data of millions of people.

- **Present Day: Expanding Threat Landscape and Evolving Tactics -** Ransomware attacks, supply chain assaults, social engineering, state-sponsored hacking, and cyberattacks on vital infrastructure are just a few of the crimes that define the current cyber threat landscape. Figure 1.2 represents History and timeline of international industrial control system (ICS) cyberattacks.
-

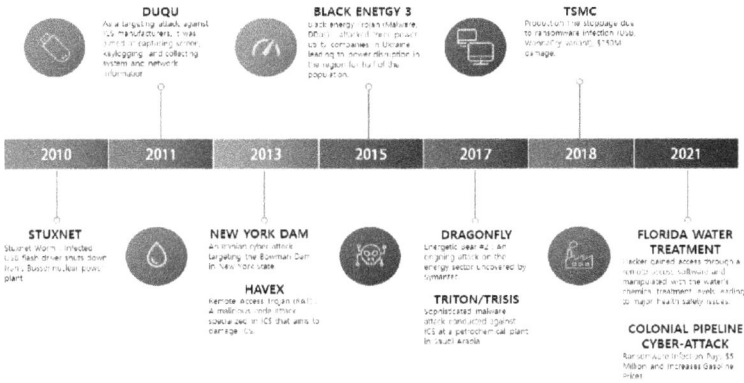

Figure 1.2 History and timeline of international industrial control system (ICS) cyberattacks (Kim & Lee, 2022).

As technology develops, cybercrime keeps changing and presenting serious problems for people, businesses, and governments. To prevent and lessen cyber risks, regulatory frameworks, international cooperation, public awareness campaigns, and ongoing advancements in cybersecurity measures are all necessary in the fight against cybercrime.

Property laws have changed to address cybercrime, but how property rights are applied in the digital sphere might differ from how they are in the physical world. Electronic communications are protected by privacy laws, yet people and artists have rights in their digital creations that are comparable to those of property owners. The scales may, however, tip in favor of law enforcement when these communications are found to be significant in a criminal investigation, when property-based analysis may produce different results. In the digital era, there is a complicated and continuing legal and ethical dispute over how to strike a balance between security and privacy.

For instance, copyright infringement in the digital era is addressed by the DMCA. It grants content producers the sole authority to decide how their digital works are used. These rights are comparable to those of owners of tangible property, including the prohibition on unauthorized use or duplication.

Compared to copyrighted works, electronic communications—such as emails and digital messages—are handled differently. People have a legitimate expectation that their internet conversations will remain private. Laws like the Electronic Communications Privacy Act (ECPA), which imposes limitations on accessing and intercepting electronic communications, safeguard it.

The legal analysis may change when electronic communications are examined in a criminal inquiry. Electronic communications may be sought after by law enforcement as evidence in a criminal prosecution. Conflicts between the right to privacy and the necessity of looking into and stopping cybercrimes can occasionally result from it.

The claim that a "property-based analysis leads in exactly the opposite direction" in criminal investigations may allude to the possibility that in certain situations, granting access for investigative reasons will take precedence over safeguarding private rights. For the sake of law enforcement, property rights may occasionally be suspended, particularly in cases where there is a plausible suspicion of criminal behavior.

1.5 Different Kinds of Cybercrime

Cybercrime encompasses criminal activities conducted using computers, networks, and the internet.

- **Malware** - Malicious software aims to harm systems or data or get unauthorized access, such as worms, Trojan horses, spyware, adware, and ransomware.

- **Phishing -** Through emails, websites, or conversations, deceptive approaches pose as a reputable business and fool people into disclosing critical information.
- **Identity Theft -** Stealing personal data to carry out crimes like money theft, fraud, or other crimes.
- **Cyber Fraud -** fraudulent actions to make money, including lotto, credit card, investment, and internet banking fraud.
- **Denial of Service (DoS) and Distributed Denial of Service (DDoS) Attacks -** overloading a server or network to the point where users can't access a service or website, causing disruptions to business operations.
- **Ransomware Attacks -** It encrypts data or systems and requests payment using bitcoin for the decryption key.
- **Social Engineering -** Manipulating people using different psychological tricks to reveal private information.
- **Cyberbullying -** This attack targets people, especially kids, by using digital communication channels to harass, threaten, or intimidate them.
- **Online Child Exploitation -** Children are sexually abused and exploited over the internet, especially through child pornography and grooming.
- **Insider Threats -** In this attack, malicious activities are conducted by individuals with authorized access to systems.
- **Credit Card Skimming -** Unauthorized capture of credit card information during a legitimate transaction, usually at point-of-sale terminals or ATMs.
- **Cyber Espionage -** Unauthorized access to computer systems or networks to obtain confidential or sensitive information for political, economic, or competitive advantage.
- **Hacking-** Unauthorized access to computer systems or networks to manipulate, steal, destroy data, or disrupt operations.
- **Cryptojacking-** Illegitimate use of someone else's computer or device to mine cryptocurrencies without their knowledge or consent.
- **Spam and Email Fraud -** Sending unsolicited emails, often containing deceptive content, scams, or malicious attachments or links.

- **Man-in-the-Middle (MitM) Attacks - It is** Intercepting and altering communications between two parties without their knowledge, enabling eavesdropping or data manipulation.
- **Data Breaches -It is an** Unauthorized access to and extraction of sensitive data from databases or systems. It results in the exposure of personal and financial information.
- **Software Piracy -** Illegally distributing or using software without proper licensing or authorization.

Cybercriminals continually adapt and innovate their tactics, making it essential for individuals, organizations, and governments to stay vigilant and employ comprehensive cybersecurity measures to protect against these varied cyber threats.

1.6 Researching Cyberlaws

Cyber laws are legal regulations and statutes designed to address and govern issues related to digital communication, computers, and online activities. These laws help establish guidelines, rights, responsibilities, and penalties concerning various aspects of cyberspace. On the other hand, cybercrimes refer to illegal activities using computers, networks, or digital devices to commit fraudulent or harmful acts. Cyber laws aim to deter and prosecute cyber crimes effectively. Understanding and enforcing cyber laws is crucial to combat cybercrimes effectively, protect individuals and organizations, and maintain a secure digital environment.

Cyber laws:
- **Computer Fraud and Abuse Act (CFAA)** *(Kerr, 2009)* **(USA)-** It is a legal framework to address unauthorized access to computers and related systems.
- *Electronic Communications Privacy Act (ECPA) (Doyle, 2011) (USA)- It protects electronic communications from interception or unauthorized access and regulates government access to stored wire and electronic communications.*
- *General Data Protection Regulation (GDPR) (Regulation, 2018) (EU) - It Regulates the collection, use, storage, and*

sharing of personal data within the European Union (EU) and European Economic Area (EEA).
- **California Consumer Privacy Act (CCPA)** *(Pardau, 2018)**(USA)- It g*rants California residents specific rights over their personal information and imposes obligations on businesses regarding data privacy and security.
- **Information Technology Act (IT Act) (India)-** *It addresses various cybercrimes, including unauthorized access, hacking, identity theft, and cyberbullying, and provides legal provisions for digital signatures and electronic records.*
- **Cybercrime Prevention Act (RA 10175) (Philippines) –** *It focusses on cybercrimes such as illegal access, data interference, system interference, cybersex, and content-related offenses.*
- **Cybersecurity Law (China) –** *The law mandates data localization and requires security assessments for critical network infrastructure and establishes requirements for network operators to ensure cybersecurity.*

1.7 Cybercrime Investigation

Cybercrime investigation identifies, analyzes, and responds to criminal activities conducted in the digital realm. These investigations aim to gather evidence, attribute the cybercrime to individuals or groups, and support legal actions to hold perpetrators accountable. Here's a general overview of the steps and components involved in a cybercrime investigation:
- **Report and Initial Assessment:** Begin with receiving a report or identifying suspicious activity that may indicate a cybercrime. Evaluate the nature and severity of the incident.
- **Preservation of Evidence:** Secure and preserve digital evidence to prevent loss, alteration, or tampering. Use forensically sound practices and tools to create a forensic image of affected systems.
- **Identification and Categorization:** Determine the type of cybercrime, such as hacking, phishing, malware attack, identity theft, etc. Categorize the incident based on its characteristics.

- **Forensic Analysis:** Conduct a thorough forensic analysis of the digital evidence, including examining files, system logs, network traffic, and other relevant data. Utilize specialized tools and techniques to extract, interpret, and correlate information.
- **Attribution and Profiling:** Attempt to identify the cybercriminal or group responsible for the crime by analyzing patterns, tactics, techniques, and motivations. Profiling may involve understanding the intent and capabilities of the attacker.
- **Incident Remediation:** Take necessary actions to contain the incident, remove malware, restore affected systems, and implement security measures to prevent further damage.
- **Documentation and Chain of Custody:** Document all actions taken during the investigation, maintain a chain of custody for evidence, and ensure evidence is admissible in court.
- **Collaboration with Law Enforcement:** Coordinate with law enforcement agencies to report cybercrime, provide evidence, and support legal proceedings.
- **Legal and Prosecutorial Involvement:** Work closely with legal authorities to build a case against the perpetrator, testify in court as necessary, and assist in cybercriminal.
- **Post-Investigation Review and Recommendations** – It Conducts a post-mortem analysis of the investigation, identify lessons learned, and make recommendations to enhance cybersecurity and prevent future incidents.
- **Victim Support and Communication:** - Communicate with affected parties, provide guidance, and support victims in understanding the incident and mitigating its impact.

Cybercrime investigations require specialized knowledge, skills, and collaboration between law enforcement, digital forensics experts, legal professionals, and cybersecurity specialists. It investigates cybercrimes, brings the perpetrators to justice, and mitigates the risks and damages associated with such incidents.

1.8 Factors Affecting Cybercrime

Cybercrime is influenced by various factors. Understanding these factors is crucial for developing effective strategies to prevent, combat, and mitigate cyber threats.

- **Technological Advancements:** It is Rapid advancements in technology provide cybercriminals with new tools and techniques to exploit vulnerabilities, making it easier to launch sophisticated cyber-attacks.
- **Anonymity and Pseudonymity:** The ability to remain anonymous or use pseudonyms while engaging in online activities makes it challenging to trace cybercriminals, encouraging illegal behavior.
- **Global Reach and Connectivity:** The internet's global reach allows cybercriminals to target victims worldwide, crossing international borders, and making it difficult to prosecute them under a single jurisdiction.
- **Lack of Cybersecurity Awareness:** Insufficient knowledge about cybersecurity and the potential risks associated with online activities can lead individuals and organizations to underestimate the importance of implementing security measures, making them more susceptible to cyber-attacks.
- **Economic Incentives:** Cybercrime can be highly profitable, attracting individuals and organized criminal groups seeking financial gains through activities - ransomware, identity theft, credit card fraud, and more.
- **Insufficient Regulations and Enforcement:** Gaps or inadequacies in cyber-related laws and regulations can create a conducive environment for cybercriminals, as they may perceive the legal consequences as minor or unlikely.
- **Weak Cybersecurity Measures:** Poorly secured systems, lack of regular updates, and inadequate cybersecurity measures provide cybercriminals with easier targets for exploitation and unauthorized access.
- **Sophisticated Cyber-Attack Tools:** Availability and easy access to sophisticated hacking tools in the underground market empower even less skilled individuals to carry out cyber-attacks.

- **Hacktivism and Ideological Motives:** Cyber-attacks driven by political, ideological, or social motives, known as hacktivism, can lead individuals or groups to engage in cyber-crimes to promote their beliefs, disrupt operations, or raise awareness.
- **Social Engineering and Manipulation:** Cybercriminals exploit human psychology through techniques like phishing, pretexting, and baiting to deceive individuals and gain unauthorized access to systems or information.
- **Opportunistic Exploitation:** Cybercriminals often exploit emerging events, vulnerabilities, or trends, such as natural disasters, global health crises, or popular topics, to launch attacks that capitalize on public interest and fear.
- **Supply Chain Vulnerabilities:** Weaknesses in the supply chain, including third-party vendors and partners, can be exploited by cybercriminals to infiltrate target organizations and gain unauthorized access to systems and data.
- **Increased Use of Cryptocurrencies:** The use of cryptocurrencies for transactions in cybercrimes, due to its pseudonymous nature, adds complexity to tracking financial transactions and can aid in evading law enforcement.

Understanding these factors and continuously adapting cybersecurity strategies and policies are essential to effectively combat cybercrime and protect individuals, organizations, and society at large.

1.9 Need for Cybersecurity

Cybersecurity is crucial in today's digitally connected world of multitude reasons that highlight the need to protect individuals, organizations, and societies from cyber threats and attacks.
- **Protecting Sensitive Data -** Cybersecurity safeguards sensitive personal, financial, medical, and business data from unauthorized access, theft, or misuse, ensuring privacy and confidentiality.
- **Preventing Financial Loss-** Effective cybersecurity measures help prevent financial fraud, unauthorized transactions, and other cybercrimes that can result in significant monetary losses for individuals and organizations.

- **Safeguarding Intellectual Property-** Intellectual property, including trade secrets, patents, and proprietary technologies, is a valuable asset for businesses. Cybersecurity helps protect these assets from theft or unauthorized access.
- **Ensuring Business Continuity-** Cybersecurity measures, including disaster recovery and business continuity planning, help organizations maintain operations in the face of cyber-attacks or other disruptions, minimizing downtime and losses.
- **Maintaining Customer Trust** -Customers trust organizations to protect their data. Cybersecurity breaches can erode trust and damage a company's reputation, leading to customer loss and reduced market share.
- **Compliance with Regulations -** Many industries are subject to legal and regulatory requirements regarding data protection. Adhering to cybersecurity standards ensures compliance with relevant laws and regulations.
- **Counteracting Cyber Threats -** Cyber threats are continually evolving and becoming more sophisticated. Effective cybersecurity measures are necessary to stay ahead of cybercriminals and protect against emerging threats.
- **Preventing Identity Theft -** Cybersecurity helps mitigate identity theft, where cybercriminals steal personal information to impersonate individuals for financial or other malicious purposes.
- **Supporting National Security -** Cyber-attacks can target critical infrastructure, government systems, or defense networks. Strong cybersecurity measures are essential for national security and defense against cyber threats.
- **Securing IoT Devices -** The proliferation of Internet of Things (IoT) devices presents additional attack vectors. Cybersecurity is vital to protect these devices and prevent potential exploitation.
- **Mitigating Ransomware Attacks -** Ransomware attacks encrypt data and demand a ransom for decryption. Robust cybersecurity measures help prevent these attacks and minimize the potential damage.
- **Promoting Digital Innovation and Growth -** A secure digital environment encourages innovation, fosters digital

transformation, and supports the growth of technology-driven economies.

- **Addressing Insider Threats** - Cybersecurity measures help organizations monitor and mitigate risks associated with employees, contractors, or other insiders who may pose a threat to information security.

1.10 Overview of the Book

The book covers the risks associated with cyberattacks, how to identify them, and basic security precautions to keep them at bay. Chapter 1 defines cybercrime and its evolution over time. It discusses the increasing prevalence and sophistication of cyber threats. It Introduces key historical cyber incidents that shaped the field. It details various forms of cybercrime, including malware attacks, phishing, hacking, identity theft, etc. It provides real-world examples to illustrate each type. It explores the motivations behind cybercrime, such as financial gain, hacktivism, state-sponsored attacks, and more. It discusses how technological advancements and societal changes impact cybercrime trends. It Provides an overview of the legal frameworks and regulations governing cyber activities. It discusses international cooperation and the challenges of enforcing cyber laws. chapter 2 defines cybersecurity threats and their significance in the digital landscape. It discusses the diverse range of threats, from common to advanced persistent threats (APTs). It details various threats, including malware, ransomware, social engineering, insider threats, and more. It explains how threat actors exploit vulnerabilities to compromise systems. chapter 3 introduces the importance of early threat detection in cybersecurity. It discusses the need for a multi-layered approach to detection. It explores different methods of detecting cyber threats, such as signature-based detection, anomaly detection, and behavioral analysis. It highlights the role of cybersecurity tools and technologies. It discusses the importance of a well-defined incident response plan. It details the steps involved in responding to a cybersecurity incident. chapter 4 discusses proactive measures, including encryption, access controls, and secure coding practices. It explores how organizations can reduce the attack surface. It details measures for detecting and responding to security incidents in real-time. It discusses the role of firewalls, intrusion detection/prevention systems, and security awareness training. It explores strategies for recovering from a cybersecurity incident. It discusses the importance of learning from incidents and improving security posture.

References

Doyle, C. (2011). Privacy: An overview of the electronic communications privacy act. *Congressional Research Service, Library of Congress.*

Farion-Melnyk, A., Rozheliuk, V., Slipchenko, T., & Banakh, S. F. (2021). Ransomware attacks: risks, protection and prevention measures. *11th International Conference on Advanced Computer Information Technologies (ACIT)* (pp. 473-478). Deggendorf, Germany: IEEE.

Kerr, O. S. (2009). Vagueness Challenges to the Computer Fraud and Abuse Act. *Minn. L. Rev, 94*, 1561.

Kim, H.-m., & Lee, K.-h. (2022). IIoT Malware Detection Using Edge Computing and Deep Learning for Cybersecurity in Smart Factories. *Applied Sciences, 12*(15), 7679.

Murthy, D. (2018). *Twitter.* Cambridge: Polity Press.

Orús, C., Barlés, M. J., Belanche, D., Casaló, L., Fraj, E., & Gurrea, R. (2016). The effects of learner-generated videos for YouTube on learning outcomes and satisfaction. *Computers & Education, 95*, 254-269.

Pardau, S. L. (2018). The california consumer privacy act: Towards a european-style privacy regime in the united states. *J. Tech. L. & Pol'y, 23*, 68.

Qabajeh, I., Thabtah, F., & Chiclana, F. (2018). A recent review of conventional vs. automated cybersecurity anti-phishing techniques. *Computer Science Review, 29*, 44-55.

Regulation, G. D. (2018). General data protection regulation (GDPR). *Intersoft Consulting, 24*(1).

Safitra, M., Lubis, M., & Fakhrurroja, H. (2023). Counterattacking Cyber Threats: A Framework for the Future of Cybersecurity. *Sustainability, 15*(18), 13369.

Sudhakar, & Kumar, S. (2020). An emerging threat Fileless malware: a survey and research challenges. *Cybersecurity, 3*(1), 1.

Thakur, K., & Pathan, A. S. (2020). *Cybersecurity fundamentals: a real-world perspective*. Boca Raton, Florida, United States.: CRC Press.

Thames, L., & Schaefer, D. (2017). *Cybersecurity for industry 4.0*. Heidelberg: Springer.

Van Dijck, J. (. (2013). 'You have one identity': Performing the self on Facebook and LinkedIn. *Media, culture & society, 35*(2), 199-215.

Wilson, R. E., Gosling, S. D., & Graham, L. T. (2012). A review of Facebook research in the social sciences. *Perspectives on psychological science, 7*(3), 203-220.

CHAPTER 2

THREATS TO CYBERSECURITY

Abstract

We come across several risks as we make our way through the complex web of the digital world. These threats aim to take advantage of holes in our systems, steal confidential data, and obstruct the smooth operation of our interwoven lives. This introduction explores the varied nature of the dangers we confront by giving a broad overview of the dynamic and diversified environment of cybersecurity threats. Cyber dangers are global in nature, affecting organizations of all sizes and cutting across national boundaries. The risks are many and ever-changing, ranging from state-sponsored actors coordinating elaborate operations to lone hackers using easily accessible resources. Cyber dangers are becoming more sophisticated as technology progresses. Malicious actors use a variety of strategies, from conventional malware to advanced persistent threats (APTs), which function covertly for lengthy periods. The dynamic nature of the environment is typified by the persistent appearance of new attack vectors and the flexibility of threat actors in exploiting weaknesses.

Even if technology defenses have improved, social engineering and phishing are two common tactics used by cybercriminals to target the human element. The goal of deceptive methods is to coerce people into disclosing private information, which highlights the significance of cybersecurity education and awareness. This chapter talks about different kinds of existing cyber threats.

Keywords: cyberthreats, malware, phishing, cybersecurity

2.1 Introduction

The technique of preventing theft, damage, or unauthorized access to computer systems, networks, and data is known as cybersecurity. It includes a range of tools, procedures, and methods intended to protect electronic data and uphold its availability, confidentiality, and integrity. In a world going digital and where systems and data are always in danger, cybersecurity is crucial.

Cybersecurity assaults are intentional, unapproved acts carried out by people or organizations with the bad intention of jeopardizing the security of a network, data, or computer system. These attacks come in various forms, and their common goal is to take advantage of holes in the target system.

To protect digital assets and infrastructure, effective cybersecurity solutions seek to identify, stop, and respond to assaults. To reduce the dangers brought on by cyber-attacks, it could be necessary to use firewalls, intrusion detection systems, encryption, access restrictions, and security best practices.

In the adversarial area of cybersecurity, one group of people—attackers—tries to infiltrate networks, data, and computer systems, while another group of people—defenders—tries to keep these systems safe and secure. It is vital to comprehend the strategies, methods, and incentives of opponents, which frequently calls for knowledge from the fields of sociology, criminology, and psychology.

Because cybersecurity is a multidisciplinary topic, security concerns may be approached holistically, taking into consideration the technological, human, legal, and economic components of the sector. This strategy is critical in an environment that is continuously changing and where new risks and weaknesses appear regularly. It also emphasizes how crucial it is for specialists from different domains to work together to prevent cyberattacks and safeguard digital systems and data.

2.2 Types of Threats

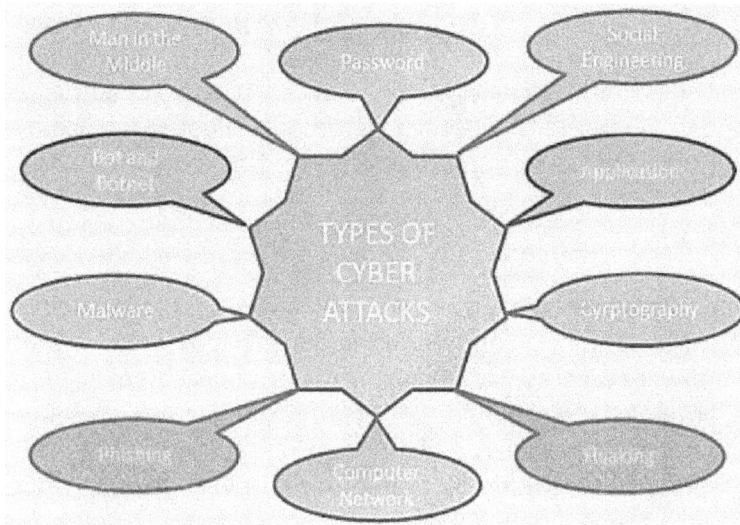

Figure 2.1 Types of attacks (Aslan, Aktuğ, Ozkan-Okay, Yilmaz, & Akin, 2023).

With the globe becoming more and more digitally linked, cybersecurity risks represent a serious and dynamic concern. Data breaches and cyberattacks are becoming more likely as technology develops and more of our private, commercial, and governmental operations take place online. Cybersecurity threats include a broad spectrum of malevolent actions and weaknesses that can jeopardize the integrity and security of data, networks, and computer systems. Figure 2.1 illustrates many assault methods.

These risks impact people, organizations, and governments globally and are not confined to any one area or business. Cyber attacks can be motivated by a variety of factors, such as political or ideological agendas, espionage, or financial gain. A successful cyberattack can have dire repercussions, such as monetary losses, harm to one's image, and even dangers to national security.

Threat actors grow more cunning as the cybersecurity landscape changes and new vulnerabilities appear. Proactive steps like software patching, personnel training, security best practices, and the usage of security technologies like firewalls, intrusion detection systems, and encryption are all necessary to defend against these attacks.

To protect their data, privacy, and operations in this linked digital world, people, organizations, and governments must recognize cybersecurity risks and put appropriate remedies in place.

2.2.1 Malware

In the field of cybersecurity, malware, which is short for "malicious software," is a ubiquitous and enduring danger. It includes a wide range of software created with the express purpose of breaking into, harming, or gaining unauthorized access to computer networks, systems, and data. Malware may take many different forms and have serious repercussions, such as system interruption, privacy violations, data theft, and financial losses.

Threat actors and cybercriminals utilize malware, a flexible and frequently hidden weapon, for a variety of nefarious purposes. It may spread via several channels, including hacked websites, malicious email attachments, and software that seems authentic.

To battle malware, cybersecurity experts utilize a range of technologies and strategies, such as intrusion detection systems, antivirus software, and user education. The danger of malware infestations may be decreased by upgrading operating systems and software regularly, exercising caution when downloading files and opening links, and maintaining strong cybersecurity practices.

Malware is a constant problem in the realm of cybersecurity because of its constant evolution. To take advantage of weaknesses and avoid detection, threat actors are always evolving and creating new malware strains. Therefore, maintaining up-to-date knowledge of malware risks and implementing strong cybersecurity defenses are essential for safeguarding digital assets and computer systems.

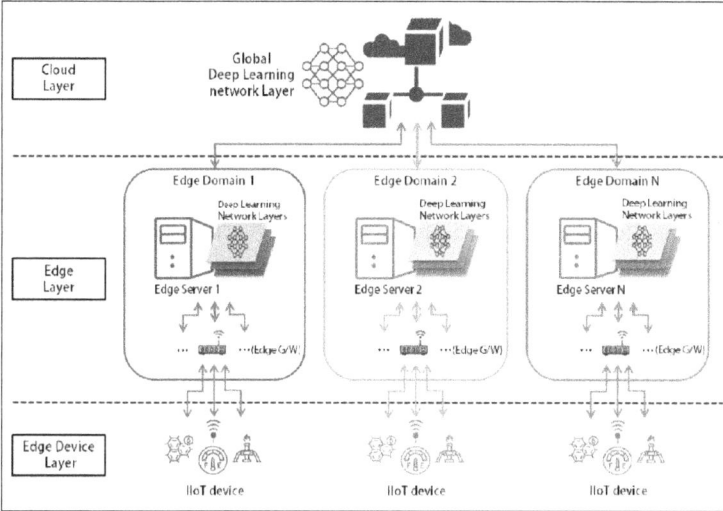

Figure 2.2 The proposed edge computing architecture for IIoT deep learning-based malware detection. (Kim & Lee, 2022).

The described system (Kim & Lee, 2022) is an architecture for deep learning-based malware detection in a smart factory environment, employing a distributed edge computing approach. The architecture consists of three layers, namely the edge device layer, the edge layer, and the cloud layer. Each layer has a specific role in the system. The Edge Device Layer comprises edge IIoT (Industrial Internet of Things) sensor terminals that are in direct contact with the data to be collected. The edge devices are embedded devices located at the network's end for collecting and processing information, such as sensors in a smart factory. The edge layer consists of several edge devices (e.g., network Router/Gateway) and edge servers. These devices and servers are responsible for performing detection using deep learning models on the local edge network. Edge devices have enough computational power to perform detection quickly. Edge servers can train deep learning models by processing local area data. Edge computing devices include a model training engine for creating classification or prediction models. Inference (malware detection) is performed by sending the model to the edge device. The cloud layer consists of a server that is responsible for training a global deep-learning model. The cloud server has superior computational power compared to the edge server, enabling training and detection with a global integrated deep learning model. The described system is a distributed edge deep learning detection method, which is different from the existing centralized deep learning malware detection method. This approach allows for local processing and detection at the edge, which can be advantageous in scenarios where real-time or low-latency processing is crucial. It involves creating and testing deep learning models. Once a model is ready, it is deployed to edge devices. Edge devices perform inference, i.e., the actual malware detection, using the deployed deep learning models. Data collected from IIoT sensors are transmitted to the edge device for analysis. Same is depicted in the Figure 2.2.

The process (Rieck, Holz, Willems, Düssel, & Laskov, 2008) described outlines a methodology used in cybersecurity for analyzing and classifying malware. It allows for the automated analysis, classification, and profiling of malware families, helping security researchers and organizations detect and respond to emerging threats and vulnerabilities in the cyber landscape. A corpus of malware binaries is collected from various sources, such as honeypots (decoy systems set up to attract attackers) and spam traps (email addresses or systems used to collect spam and malware). This corpus represents a diverse set of malware samples that are currently active in the wild. The collected malware binaries are scanned using an antivirus engine to identify known malware instances. It helps quickly identify and eliminate known threats. For the unidentified or potentially new malware, the binaries are executed and monitored in a controlled environment known as a sandbox. Sandboxing allows the analysis of the malware's behavior without compromising the host system. Any unusual or malicious activities are closely observed. During execution in the sandbox, the malware's behavior is monitored, and changes in the system state are recorded. It includes tracking API function calls, file operations, registry changes, mutex (mutual exclusion) usage, network communications, and more. Behavioral analysis helps identify patterns that are indicative of malicious behavior. Features reflecting these behavioral patterns are extracted from the analysis reports. These features might include the frequency of certain API calls, the sequence of events, or the types of files accessed or modified. These features are used to characterize the malware's behavior. The extracted features are used to create high-dimensional vectors in a vector space. Each malware sample is represented as a point in this space, where the dimensions correspond to the extracted behavioral features. This allows for quantitative analysis and comparison of malware behaviors. Machine learning techniques are applied to the high-dimensional vector space to identify shared behavioral patterns among malware families. These patterns help categorize malware into different families based on their common characteristics. Common machine learning algorithms used in this context include clustering and classification. A combined classifier is constructed based on the identified behavioral patterns. This classifier can be used to classify and categorize different malware samples into their respective families. Each malware family's discriminative model is analyzed using weight vectors that express the contribution of different behavioral patterns. These weights help understand which patterns are most significant in distinguishing one family from another. The most prominent patterns, as revealed by their weights, provide insights into the classification model. Additionally, comparing the weights across different malware families can reveal relationships and similarities between them, helping security experts better understand the landscape of malware threats.

2.2.2 Phishing

Phishing is a common and sneaky cybersecurity attack that takes advantage of human behavior through trickery and manipulation. It involves dishonest attempts to pose as a reliable organization to collect sensitive information, including credit card numbers, usernames, passwords, and personal information. Phishing assaults usually happen via email, but they can also happen through phone calls, texts, or phony websites.

Since these attacks throw a wide net to trick unsuspecting people into disclosing their personal information, the word "phishing" is derived from fishing. Phishing attacks sometimes make use of psychological traits like curiosity, fear, or haste to fool victims into doing things that endanger their security.

Phishing poses a serious risk to both individuals and organizations since it may result in identity theft, financial losses, data breaches, and reputational harm. To protect themselves from phishing attempts, people and organizations should utilize security software and email filters, educate themselves and their staff on the risks of phishing, and proceed with care when responding to unwanted emails or messages. To reduce the dangers of phishing, it is crucial to confirm the legitimacy of requests for sensitive information, such as login passwords, before answering.

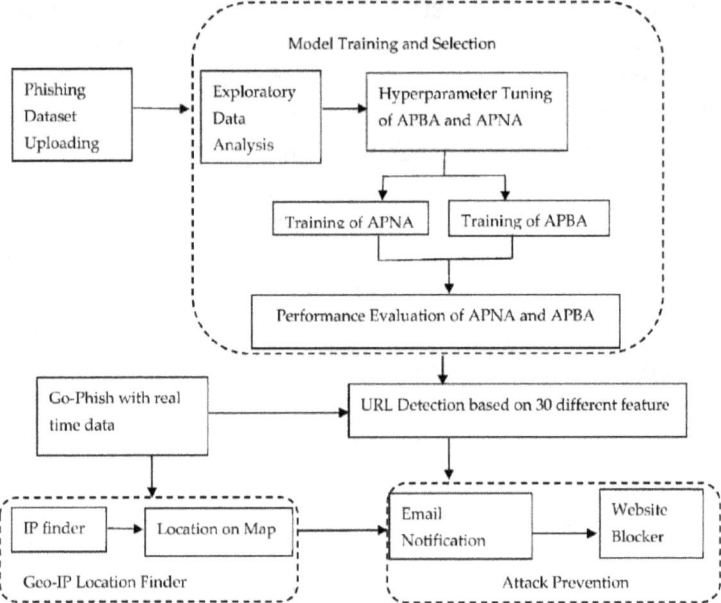

Figure 2.3 Proposed dynamic phishing safeguard system (Md, et al., 2022)

Users may learn more about a website's legitimacy and phishing tactics, where their data is going, what trackers are used on that URL, and whether or not their data is going to a reliable source by utilizing a Dynamic Phishing Safeguard System (DPSS) architecture (Md, et al., 2022). The correctness of the integrated model serves as the basis for the system's evaluation. Based on the accuracy of other models' categorization rates, the models included in DPSS are contrasted with those of similar works. Using ensemble learning techniques, the model is trained using the Anti-Phishing Boosting Algorithm. The work uses Windows 10. VS code is used as a code editor.

Python and Javascript are used as programming languages to build DPSS. Figure 2.3 represents the same.

To capture the inherent characteristics of the email text and other features to be classified as phishing or non-phishing using three different data sets, the study (Mughaid, et al., 2022) uses machine learning techniques to train a detection model. The results are then validated using test data. To get the most accurate rate, the study reprocessed the datasets after data collection by eliminating duplicate rows, eliminating missing values, and balancing the instances. 5,25,754 occurrences total in the dataset, of which 8351 are phishing emails and 5,17,402 are real emails.

To accomplish cybersecurity, a unique ODAE-WPDC model (Alqahtani, et al., 2022)is proposed and presented for the detection and categorization of WS phishing. The first step of the suggested ODAE-WPDC model involves pre-processing the input data to remove any missing values from the dataset. Feature extraction comes next, and the AAA-based FS method is applied. Lastly, the classification method uses the IWO with the DAE model.

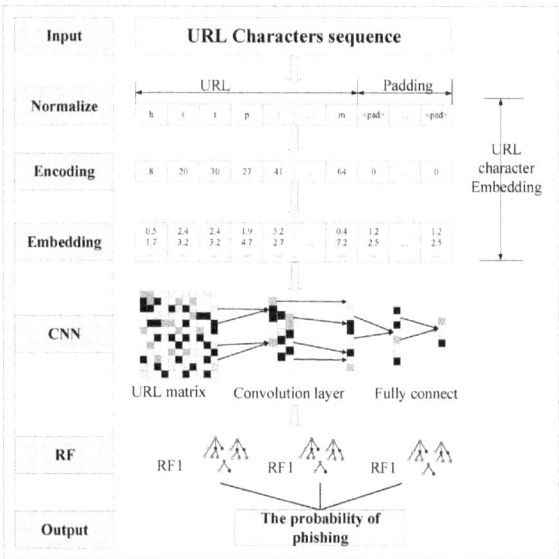

Figure 2.4 Proposed Framework (Yang, Zheng, Wu, Wu, & Wang, 2021).

There are three primary parts to the advice (Yang, Zheng, Wu, Wu, & Wang, 2021). Initially, the character embedding method is used to convert URL data into a character vector. The same data structure is included in the translated URLs, which helps identify phishing websites. Second, the model is trained using the altered URL data, and an enhanced CNN network is built. The characteristics of the various CNN network layers are obtained by extracting the URL features once the model has been trained. Third, distinct random forests are used to classify the characteristics that were taken from various network levels. The final classifier used to categorize the website is the one that yielded the best classification result. Figure 2.4 represents the same.

2.2.3 Man-in-Middle Attack

A cybersecurity vulnerability known as a "man-in-the-middle" (MitM) attack happens when an unauthorized third party monitors or intercepts communication between two parties without the parties' knowledge or approval. The attacker in question surreptitiously places oneself between the parties involved in communication, so assuming the role of an intermediary with the ability to modify or eavesdrop on the information being transferred.

MitM attacks frequently involve methods to reroute or intercept traffic, such as impersonating the DNS (Domain Name System), ARP (Address Resolution Protocol), or using proxy servers. Furthermore, SSL stripping is another tool that attackers might use to compromise encrypted communications.

Encryption solutions, such as Virtual Private Networks (VPNs) and Transport Layer Security (TLS), are necessary for mitigating MitM assaults because they safeguard data while it is in transit. Additionally, users should exercise caution when using public Wi-Fi networks and make sure that websites and digital certificates are legitimate. Keeping up with security best practices and regular software upgrades will help lower the likelihood of being a victim of MitM attacks. To combat this widespread cybersecurity danger, people and organizations must continue to be watchful and proactive.

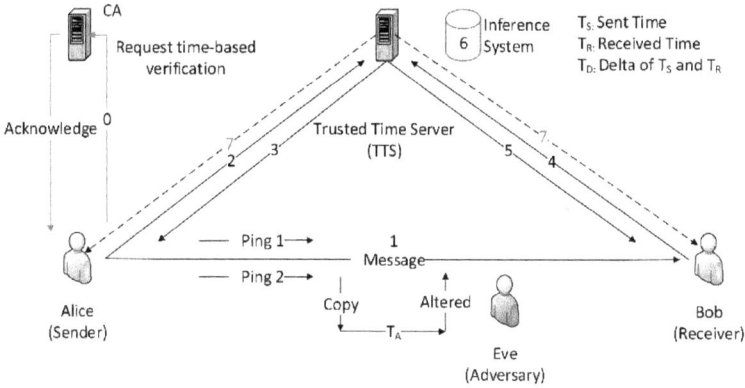

Figure 2.5 Proposed work (Kang, Fahd, & Venkatraman, 2018).

The approach (Kang, Fahd, & Venkatraman, 2018) automatically and successfully detects suspicious behaviors from MITM assaults using a time-based verification of transmission combined with an inferencing database at a TTS. To defeat the different evasive strategies that an MITM adversary may employ, it employs intelligent learning techniques.

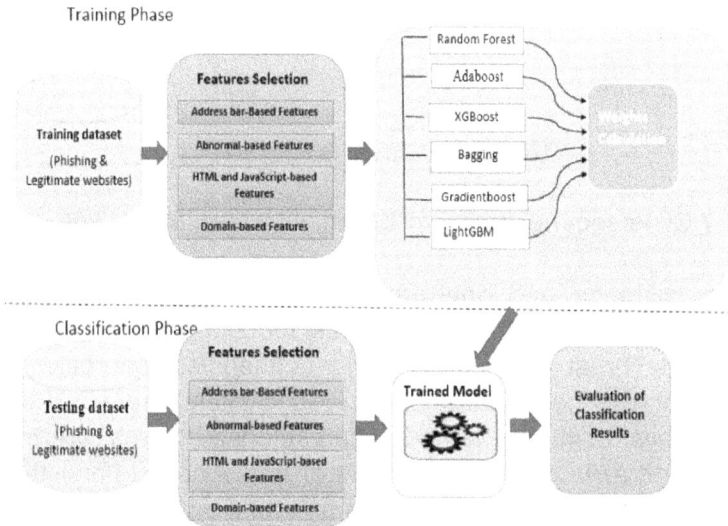

Figure 2.6 Proposed Framework (Taha, 2021).

The suggested method (Taha, 2021) is divided into two sections: First, the final classification results are based on individual

29

judgments and are produced by four heterogeneous machine-learning algorithms, known for their respective strengths and limitations. These are known as the base learners. To differentiate between phishing and authentic websites, a weighted soft voting method is employed to allocate higher weights of influence to more proficient base learners and lower weights of influence to less proficient base learners. The results of all the classifiers are then combined based on their weights. Figure 2.6 represents the same.

2.2.4 Advanced Persistent Attack

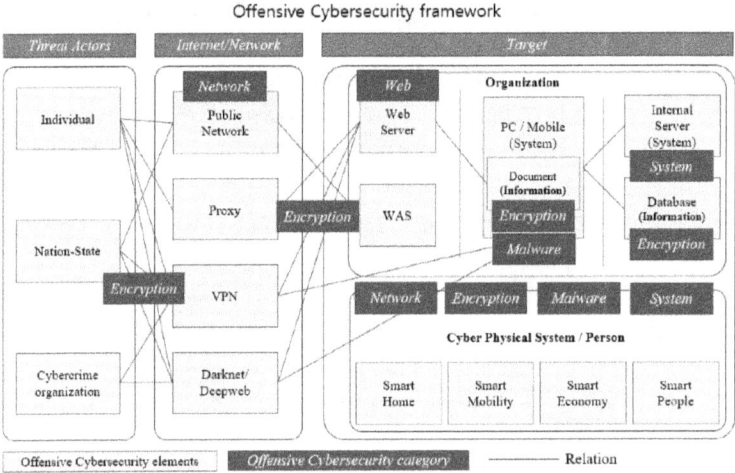

Offensive Cybersecurity framework

Figure 2.7 Cybersecurity framework (Kim, Alfouzan, & Kim, 2021).

Stealth, persistence, and long-term attention define an Advanced Persistent Threat (APT), a highly skilled and focused type of cybersecurity assault. Threat actors with significant financial resources and expertise, such as nation-state-sponsored hackers, organized cybercrime gangs, or highly trained cyberespionage teams, are frequently behind APTs. The principal aim of an Advanced Persistent Threat (APT) is to obtain unapproved entry into a designated target, sustain that entry for a prolonged duration, and steal confidential data or accomplish goals. The framework for cybersecurity is shown in Figure 2.7.

Defense against Advanced Persistent Threats (APTs) necessitates a high degree of cybersecurity readiness, ongoing attention to detail, and a thorough comprehension of the threat environment due to their intricacy and ingenuity. Entities and organizations that possess important infrastructure or valuable data should take extra precautions to guard against APTs.

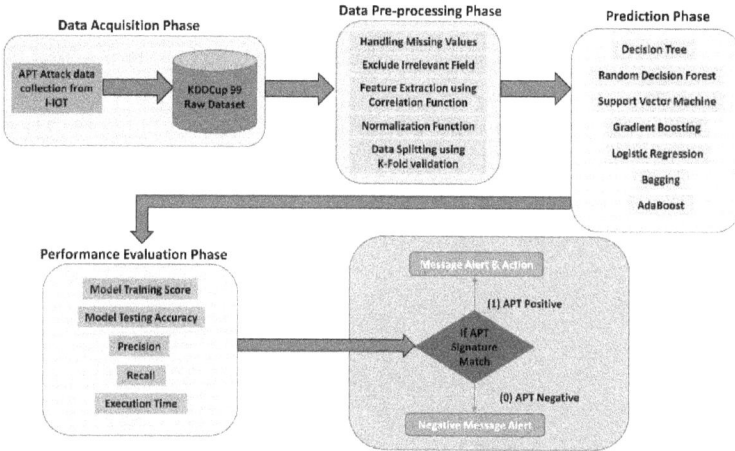

Figure 2.8 Proposed system (Javed, et al., 2022).

Using publicly accessible KDDCup99 datasets that are especially suited for the IoT sector, the work (Javed, et al., 2022) presents a unique lightweight, and fast machine learning-based APT signature classification system that can identify and forecast malicious nodes using a variety of traditional ML methods. Phases one through four comprise data collection, pre-processing, prediction, and performance evaluation. A computer with an Intel Core i7 CPU running at 1.70 GHz and 8 GB of RAM is used for simulation. Figure 2.8 represents the same.

2.2.5 Ransomware

One especially sneaky and devastating type of malware that has become well-known is ransomware. This kind of malicious software encrypts the files of the victim or locks them out of the computer system, and then it demands a ransom, usually in cryptocurrency, to unlock the system or get access back. Attacks using ransomware have the potential to cause data loss, interrupt corporate operations, and be extremely costly.

Attacks using ransomware have worried people and businesses of all kinds. A successful ransomware attack can have serious repercussions, such as monetary losses, lost revenue, interruptions to company operations, harm to one's reputation, and loss of important data. There is no assurance that the attacker will supply the decryption key, even if the ransom is paid.

Attackers using ransomware are becoming more proficient, and the assaults themselves are still evolving. A strong backup and recovery plan, together with proactive cybersecurity measures, are essential for reducing the threats brought on by ransomware.

2.2.6 DNS Attack

Cybersecurity risks known as DNS (Domain Name System) attacks target the core internet infrastructure that converts human-readable domain names (like www.example.com) into IP addresses that computers use to find web servers and other network resources. DNS assaults have the potential to interfere with, alter, or breach this vital system, affecting a variety of internet services and operations.
DNS assaults may have detrimental effects on an organization's reputation in addition to causing financial losses, data theft, and website outages. Attackers can alter users' online experiences by breaking into the DNS system, possibly sending them to phony websites or intercepting private information.

To properly fight against DNS assaults, defenders must modify their security procedures as these attacks continue to advance. Because DNS is essential to internet communication, maintaining its security is essential to the general stability and security of the online environment.

2.2.7 Denial-of-Service Attack

A cybersecurity threat known as a denial-of-service (DoS) attack seeks to prevent a targeted computer system, network, or online service from operating as usual. A denial-of-service (DoS) attack occurs when an attacker overwhelms the target with a large volume of requests, traffic, or other data, overloading the system and rendering it inoperable for authorized users. A denial-of-service (DoS) attack aims to prevent authorized users from accessing the targeted resource by making it inaccessible.

DoS assaults remain a danger to cybersecurity, and attackers are always changing their strategies. To effectively counteract such assaults, a mix of alert monitoring, quick reaction times, and proactive security measures is needed.

2.2.8 SQL Injection Attack

A cybersecurity issue known as an SQL injection attack focuses on weak points in an application's communication with a database. This attack involves inserting malicious SQL (Structured Query Language) code into user input fields or other web application components, leading the program to execute SQL queries that are not intended. An SQL injection attack aims to obtain unauthorized access to the underlying systems by manipulating, stealing, or altering data that is stored in the database.

Within online application security, SQL injection attacks remain a common and significant issue. Organizations and developers may greatly lower the likelihood of being victims of SQL injection attacks by using a proactive and multi-layered approach to application security.

2.2.9 Zero-day Exploit

A zero-day exploit is a kind of cyberattack that preys on a software flaw that the software provider is unaware of. Because they offer a window of opportunity to corrupt systems and data before the software vendor can create and issue a security patch to correct the vulnerability, zero-day exploits are widely sought after by cybercriminals and other hostile actors.

Zero-day vulnerabilities pose a serious threat to cybersecurity because they render people and organizations exposed until a fix is created and implemented. Zero-day exploit risk cannot be eliminated, but it may be lessened by proactive security measures and quick fixes for known vulnerabilities.

2.2.10 Social Engineering Attack

Cybercriminals employ social engineering, a misleading and manipulative tactic, to take advantage of people's tendency to divulge personal information or do activities that undermine security. Social engineering attacks rely on human behavior flaws, in contrast to standard cybersecurity threats that target software vulnerabilities or infrastructure weaknesses. To accomplish their goals, these attacks frequently entail psychological manipulation, impersonation, and the exploitation of trust.

Cybersecurity concerns such as identity theft, data breaches, unauthorized access, and financial fraud can all be caused by social engineering assaults.

Attacks using social engineering frequently target people, who are the weakest link in the security system. Through the integration of technology, user education, and awareness, organizations may enhance their defenses against these misleading attacks.

2.3 Challenges

As they work to safeguard their digital assets, data, and infrastructure, people, organizations, and governments face threats from cybersecurity assaults. Among the main difficulties brought on by cybersecurity threats are:
- Adapting Attack Strategies: To take advantage of weaknesses and avoid discovery, cyber criminals are always creating new and advanced attack techniques. To remain ahead

of ever-changing dangers, one must always be alert and flexible.

- Zero-Day Security Flaws: Attackers can take advantage of zero-day vulnerabilities, which are software weaknesses that have not yet been fixed. It is more difficult to identify and defend against attacks that target zero-day vulnerabilities.
- Attack Scale: Botnets and distributed denial of service (DDoS) assaults have the potential to produce enormous amounts of malicious traffic, which makes it challenging to control the damage and preserve service availability.
- Insider Threats: Since insiders frequently have authorized access to systems and data, attacks carried out by persons within an organization present serious difficulties.
- Data Breaches: Cybersecurity assaults may result in data breaches, which may have far-reaching effects such as fines and penalties from authorities, a decline in confidence, and financial difficulties.
- **Threat:** Advanced Persistent Threats (APTs) are deliberate, long-lasting attacks carried out by knowledgeable and well-funded enemies. Cutting-edge security techniques are needed to recognize and address APTs.
- **Resource Restrictions:** Many businesses, especially smaller ones, struggle with a lack of staff, funding, and cybersecurity knowledge.
- **User Awareness:** Successful assaults frequently stem from human mistakes. Although difficult, educating consumers about cybersecurity dangers and acceptable practices is crucial.
- The global nature of threats makes international collaboration and attack attribution challenging since cyber threats might come from anywhere in the globe.
- **Regulations and Compliance:** It may be difficult to comply with legal and regulatory requirements for cybersecurity and data protection, particularly when those requirements change over time.
- **Encryption:** Although encryption is essential for safeguarding data, hackers can utilize it to conceal harmful behavior. Finding a balance between privacy and security is difficult.

- **Supply Chain Attacks:** Vulnerabilities in commonly used goods might arise from an attacker's breach of the software or hardware supply chain.
- **Quick Technological Advancements:** As technology develops, new attack avenues and vulnerabilities appear. It's never easy to make sure security precautions stay up with technological advancements.
- **Timeliness** - Effectively responding to a cybersecurity event may be difficult as it calls for prompt detection and containment of the breach, as well as investigation and recovery—often under time constraints.
- **Advanced Technologies**: It might be difficult to identify and counteract assaults that are enhanced by the use of artificial intelligence and machine learning by attackers.
- **Lack of Standardisation:** Cybersecurity defenses may become inconsistent due to a lack of industry-wide security policies and procedures.
- **Geopolitical Factors**: State-sponsored cyberattacks and geopolitical conflicts can make cybersecurity issues worse.

A thorough and proactive strategy for cybersecurity is required to address these issues, one that incorporates risk assessment, security awareness, cutting-edge tools and technology, and a robust incident response plan. Reducing the effect of cybersecurity assaults requires cooperation within the cybersecurity community, exchange of threat intelligence, and adaptation to the ever-evolving threat landscape.

2.4 Future Scope

Cybersecurity threats are anticipated to continue developing in the future, posing new and increasingly difficult problems for people, businesses, and governments. The following are some future trends and projections for cybersecurity attacks:
- Increasing Automation and AI: To improve their assaults, cybercriminals are likely to make use of automation and artificial intelligence. It involves automating vulnerability detection and malware optimization using machine learning.

- Smart Device and IoT Vulnerabilities: Smart gadgets and the Internet of Things (IoT) will increase in popularity, opening up new attack vectors and giving hackers the chance to penetrate vital infrastructure, commercial buildings, and residential areas.
- Risks associated with 5G and Edge Computing: The deployment of 5G networks and the use of edge computing will bring up new weaknesses and difficulties.
- Supply Chain Assaults: It is anticipated that supply chain assaults will increase in frequency as hackers target the hardware and software supply chains to compromise commonly used goods.
- Dangers of Quantum Computing: Post-quantum cryptography is required to protect data since the emergence of quantum computing has the potential to undermine existing encryption techniques.
- Evolution of Ransomware: More focused and devastating ransomware assaults are probably ahead of us. Attackers could threaten to reveal confidential data and demand larger ransom payments.
- Biometric Spoofing: With the increasing use of biometric authentication systems, hackers can create new ways to trick or undermine biometric security.
- Challenges with Cloud Security: Attackers will focus more on cloud environment security as people depend more on cloud services, particularly in multi-cloud and hybrid cloud infrastructures.
- AI-Enhanced Cybersecurity: Although hackers could utilize AI for malevolent intent, businesses will utilize AI more and more for threat identification, mitigation, and incident handling.
- Deepfakes and Manipulated Material: Social engineering and misinformation campaigns can be aided by the employment of deepfake technology and manipulated material, which erodes credibility.
- Nation-State Attacks: Given that geopolitical conflicts frequently seep into cyberspace, state-sponsored cyberattacks are likely to continue. Multinational businesses,

governments, and vital infrastructure might be the targets of these attacks.

- Privacy Concerns: As laws like the California Consumer Privacy Act (CCPA) and the General Data Protection Regulation (GDPR) require more data protection, striking a balance between security and privacy concerns is becoming more and more difficult.
- Changes in Regulation and Compliance: Tighter rules and sanctions for noncompliance are anticipated as the cybersecurity regulatory environment changes.
- Attackers will persist in taking advantage of social engineering tactics and human psychology through user education and human-centric attacks. Improving user awareness and education will be essential to defense.
- Cybersecurity Workforce Shortages: It is anticipated that there will remain a deficiency of qualified cybersecurity specialists, which will make it challenging for enterprises to assemble and retain robust security teams.

A mix of cutting-edge technology, threat information sharing, proactive security measures, and a focus on a cybersecurity culture will be needed to remain ahead of cybersecurity threats as the digital world continues to change. Adaptability to new threats and technological advancements will be essential for future-proof cybersecurity.

References

Alqahtani, H., Alotaibi, S., Alrayes, F., Al-Turaiki, I., Alissa, K., Aziz, A., . . . Al Duhayyim, M. (2022). Evolutionary Algorithm with Deep Auto Encoder Network Based Website Phishing Detection and Classification. *Applied Sciences, 12*(15), 7441.

Aslan, Ö., Aktuğ, S., Ozkan-Okay, M., Yilmaz, A., & Akin, E. (2023). A Comprehensive Review of Cyber Security Vulnerabilities, Threats, Attacks, and Solutions. *Electronics, 12*(6), 1333.

Kang, J., Fahd, K., & Venkatraman, S. (2018). Trusted Time-Based Verification Model for Automatic Man-in-the-Middle Attack Detection in Cybersecurity. *Cryptography, 2*(4), 38.

Kim, H.-m., & Lee, K.-h. (2022). IIoT Malware Detection Using Edge Computing and Deep Learning for Cybersecurity in Smart Factories. *Applied Sciences, 12*(15), 7679.

Md, A., Jaiswal, D., Daftari, J., Haneef, S., Iwendi, C., & Jain, S. (2022). Efficient Dynamic Phishing Safeguard System Using Neural Boost Phishing Protection. *Electronics, 11*(19), 3133.

Mughaid, A., AlZu'bi, S., Hnaif, A., Taamneh, S., Alnajjar, A., & El-soud, E. A. (2022). An intelligent cyber security phishing detection system using deep learning techniques. *Cluster Computing, 25*(6), 3819-3828.

Rieck, K., Holz, T., Willems, C., Düssel, P., & Laskov, P. (2008). Learning and classification of malware behavior. *International Conference on Detection of Intrusions and Malware, and Vulnerability Assessment* (pp. 108-125). Paris, France: Heidelberg: Springer Berlin.

Yang, R., Zheng, K., Wu, B., Wu, C., & Wang, X. (2021). Phishing Website Detection Based on Deep Convolutional Neural Network and Random Forest Ensemble Learning. *Sensors, 21*(24), 8281.

CHAPTER 3

METHODOLOGIES USED TO DETECT THREATS

Abstract

A thorough cybersecurity plan must include cybersecurity detection as a crucial element to quickly identify and counteract any possible threats or assaults. A wide range of detection techniques, including signature-based, behavioral analysis, anomaly detection, and the integration of artificial intelligence and machine learning, are necessary due to the complexity of contemporary cyber threats. In summary, given the always-changing nature of cyber threats, security professionals must collaborate, continuously improve and take a proactive and adaptive approach to cybersecurity detection. This chapter details different methos used to detect the attacks.

Keywords: Cyber forensic, malware, offences, cyber threat, detection

3.1 Introduction

Protecting computer systems, networks, and data from hostile activity requires cybersecurity (Kim, et al., 2023) (Singer & Friedman, 2014) detection (Ambika N. , 2022). Early threat detection, incident response, continuous monitoring, and vulnerability management are the main goals. To identify and mitigate security risks, a variety of techniques are used, including machine learning and artificial intelligence (AI), behavioral analysis, anomaly detection, signature-based detection, and more. Handling privacy issues, adjusting to the changing threat landscape, and handling false positives are some of the challenges in cybersecurity detection. All things considered, a successful cybersecurity detection plan needs a mix of tools, ongoing observation, and knowledgeable staff to proactively detect and address possible security problems.

3.2 Attack Detection

It is crucial to keep an eye on network traffic, endpoints, and system behavior to identify anomalies from the norm and stay ahead of growing threats. Although detection systems are essential for spotting possible security events, well-trained cybersecurity personnel and efficient incident response strategies are just as important for containing, eliminating, and recovering from assaults.

The dynamic nature of the threat landscape, false positives, and privacy issues are just a few of the challenges that make it necessary to carefully balance efficiency and accuracy. To develop a robust defense against cyber attacks, organizations need to make investments in remaining up to speed on the latest dangers, modifying their detection techniques, and attending to privacy concerns.

3.3 Alert Correlation

The foundation of any defense against cyberattacks is cybersecurity alert correlation, which provides a thoughtful and deliberate method for managing the plethora of security warnings produced by contemporary systems. This procedure takes care of the problems that come with controlling the number of warnings, cutting down on false positives, and giving prospective security events contextualized knowledge.

By effectively allocating their resources, cybersecurity teams may improve incident reaction times and lessen the impact of security breaches. This is made possible by their ability to prioritize and concentrate on the most significant threats. A thorough and flexible method of alert correlation is ensured by the combination of automated tools—often found in Security Information and Event Management (SIEM) systems—with manual analysis performed by cybersecurity specialists.

Obstacles include the difficulty of combining various security systems and the requirement for precise threat intelligence highlighting how dynamic the cybersecurity environment is. Organizations must modify correlation rules, remain on top of new hazards, and adjust to changes in their IT environments to achieve continuous improvement, which is not only a goal but a must.

In the end, the correlation of cybersecurity alerts is a crucial component of a proactive and robust cybersecurity approach. It gives organizations the ability to handle the complexities of contemporary cyber threats, enabling prompt and efficient responses to security crises. The function of alert correlation is still essential in preserving the security and integrity of digital assets as cyber threats continue to change. Figure 3.1 represents Taxonomy of Alert correlation.

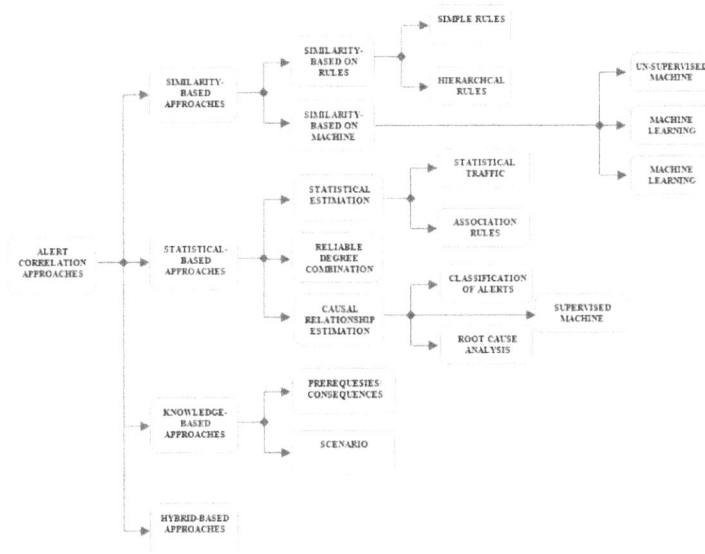

Figure 3.1 Taxonomy of Alert correlation (Albasheer, et al., 2022).

The suggested technique models (Khosravi & Ladani, 2020), finds, and analyses causal links among APT stages to compute the infection score of hosts. The study finds likely IKCs against the specified hosts by doing a causal analysis of the meta-alerts produced by security and non-security sensors. After assigning a score to each IKC for their involvement in an APT assault against the relevant host, a normalized attack surface value is calculated for each host to indicate its likelihood of becoming the target of an APT attack.

The article (Wu & Moon, 2019) presents an alert correlation technique based on attribute- and temporal-based similarity studies. To facilitate the reporting and correlation of physical alarms with cyber alterations, a new physical intrusion detection alert (PIDA) format and intrusion detection message exchange format (IDMEF) are presented. For cyber-physical alert correlations in CMS, a five-step alert correlation procedure has been designed. The temporal- and attribute-based similarity analyses are defined independently to realize each purpose. The characteristics are determined in light of prior studies on network alert correlation and current physical-based intrusion detection techniques in the industrial sector.

The TSS prototype (Pontes, Guelfi, Kofuji, & Silva, 2011) was used in a wired local area network (LAN), more precisely in a computer that served as an Internet gateway. There are many operating systems and unfiltered Internet connectivity, as well as virtualized operating systems via VMware. The Network IDPS (Snort) and logs from the gateway's operating system can be used to register alarms. The computers that carried out the assaults are represented by the IP source addresses.

The new framework called A Comprehensive System for Analysing Intrusion Alerts (ACSAnIA) (Shittu, Healing, Ghanea-Hercock, Bloomfield, & Rajarajan, 2015) is the recommendation. A unique way of grouping events using correlation information and a new prioritization measure based on anomaly detection are two of the post-correlation strategies. Using data from a 2012 cyber range experiment conducted by industry partners of the British Telecom SATURN initiative, the paper assessed the post-correlation procedures of ACSAnIA. The British Telecom SATURN Research Team has built an existing Visual Analytic tool for the examination of cyber security data, and this tool is being integrated with the proposed framework.

To attain a greater detection rate with fewer false positives, an enhanced "requires/provides" model (Alserhani, Akhlaq, Awan, & Cullen, 2010) is provided. This model establishes cooperation between statistical and knowledge-based models. After creating a correlation between attack signatures, the suggested model was effectively applied in real-time and produced security events. An organized, multi-stage operation, a botnet assault requires a complete picture of the attacker's behavior to be detected. The first step of infection entails looking for systems that are responding to backdoors or executing susceptible services. Using one or more of the various attack vectors, software is installed, and remote malicious code is injected onto the target system. The real Botnet software is directed to be downloaded by the compromised system from a specialized Bot server. After that, the malware is run, adding the machine to the botnet. Through C&C channels over HTTP or IRC, the compromised system establishes a connection with the attacker and receives orders to be updated and configured. Scanning operations identify vulnerable and unpatched systems that might harbor further infections. The attacker instructs the Botnet members to download binaries, establish a connection with a different C&C server, and launch attacks on more victims based on the capabilities of the target system.

Two innovative techniques to alert correlation are suggested in the suggestion (Granadillo, El-Barbori, & Debar, 2016). The first is predicated on models of defender capabilities and policy enforcement, while the second is predicated on information security indicators. The goal of the enforcement-based correlation approach is to extract correlation rules from the configuration of the policy enforcement points (PEPs). PEPs serve as front doors or gatekeepers for digital resources. A security decision is requested, the access decision is enforced, and the PEP describes the user's characteristics to the Policy Decision Point (PDP) when a user seeks to access a particular resource on a computer network or server.

Rather than using periods and hyper-alerts, the suggested approach (Zhang, Zhao, Luo, Xin, & Zhu, 2019)employed a novel way of organizing raw alerts based on the idea of intrinsic strong connections. Finally, a correlation graph is created by merging the pruned sessions, and based on the correlation graph, a prediction method for the upcoming attack is suggested. This process identifies highly stable correlations between actions by eliminating redundant actions and action link modes from sessions using a pruning algorithm to lessen the impact of false positives. The modeling phase and the extraction phase are the two primary phases of the IACF framework. The framework extracts intrusion activities and sessions during the extraction phase. The sessions that were extracted during the extraction phase are used to build the correlation graph during the modeling phase.

Utilizing the Java programming language, the framework operates on a server that has Windows 10 installed with 8GB RAM and a 2.6GHz Intel CPU.

3.4 Threat hunting

A proactive and calculated method of locating and reducing any security risks within a company's network or systems is called cybersecurity threat hunting. Threat hunting is a strategy in cybersecurity that differs from standard defense-oriented approaches by actively looking for indications of harmful activity that automated security technologies might have missed. Finding and removing risks before they have a chance to do serious harm is the aim.

A system called THREATRAPTOR (Gao, et al., 2021) uses OSCTI to make threat hunting in computer systems easier. gathers system-level audit records about system calls from the OS kernel by using established system auditing mechanisms. System events that detail how different system entities interact are included in the gathered kernel audit logs and are essential for security research. It derives a collection of properties that are essential for security research by parsing the gathered audit logs of system calls into a timeline of system events involving system entities. To preserve the system audit logging data, it keeps the parsed system entities and system events in databases. Before being stored in databases, the data is shrunk to optimize search performance while maintaining the integrity of vital information on malevolent activity.

One of the various applications for Sysmon and cyber threat intelligence is illustrated in this study (Mavroeidis & Jøsang, 2018). Specifically, we describe a threat assessment system based on the analysis of Sysmon log streams and a cyber threat intelligence ontology to automatically classify executable software into distinct danger levels. It developed the ontology using an agile methodology and the web ontology language (OWL). The knowledge base is subjected to inference and consistency checks using OWL constructs. Because CTIO is modular, it may leverage pre-existing ontologies and add new ideas to the core ontology skeleton with little effort on the part of the integration process. GitHub has documentation and infor-mation on CTIO.

A threat-hunting case study (Miazi, Pritom, Shehab, Chu, & Wei, 2017) is the recommendation. A variety of log data sets are provided to the participants. They are expected to use the data to determine which dangers exist. It produced data from employee authentication logs for C0mp@ny, a corporation. Every employee connects to their workplace computer every working day. Employees with the right login information and a secure connection may access their ac-counts from either their home or place of business. They have ac-cess to documents that have been shared with them or to which they have been granted permission to access. They have access to gadg-ets and other business resources. The GPS coordinates from where the employee is logged in, actions taken, devices accessed, and login and logout times are all recorded by the system.

The goal of the ICS Threat Hunting Framework (ICS-THF) (Jadidi & Lu, 2021) is to identify cyber threats against Industrial Control Systems (ICS) devices early in the attack lifecycle. Threat hunting triggers, threat hunting, and cyber threat intelligence are the three phases that makeup ICS-THF. Events or outside resources that have the po-tential to start the hunting stage are identified in the threat-hunting trigger stage. During the hunting stage, an intrusion analysis model called the Diamond model and the MITRE ATT&CK Matrix are used to create a hunting hypothesis and forecast the adversary's future ac-tions. The hypothesis that has been verified will proceed to the CTI phase to extract significant characteristics and produce adversarial signatures.

According to this study (Sree, Koganti, Kalyana, & Anudeep, 2021), threat hunting is an ecosystem's helpful, analyst-driven method of looking for an attacker's TTP. Several threats have been used to test the model on real-world data sets. Through risk hunts, the useful-ness and efficacy of this study have been demonstrated both with and without a blueprint. To emphasize the impact of this model on threat hunting in a simulated environment, the paper also provides an examination of the idea of threat hunting based on data from Ukrainian electrical grid assaults in an online setting. The analysis's conclusions include a methodical and efficient approach to locating and measuring rigor, honesty, and coverage.

The Mitre Institute maintains the ATT&CK framework (Neto & dos Santos, 2020), a knowledge base of adversary tactics and techniques based on actual observations. As of the current enterprise version 8, there are 14 tactics in the framework, which group many methods and sub-techniques inside each. The suggested architecture links ATT&CK, sigma rules, and cyber security log events to enable the durability of collected data.

The data collectors, who are in charge of obtaining data to feed the entire system (Lozano, Llopis, & Domingo, 2023), are located in the first layer. The other parts of the system will process the data when it has been gathered and saved. The database will hold the information that the collectors have collected. Massive volumes of data are being generated and collected by the entire system every second. Threat Hunters have a tough time doing their jobs since they can't analyze all the info at the appropriate rate. This study suggests automating the process of data tagging using machine learning (ML) to assist Threat Hunters in managing such enormous volumes of data. Experts in threat hunting and machine learning should be able to communicate with the system as a whole through a straightforward, attractive, and user-friendly graphical user interface that provides access to all necessary tools and visualizations. Through the use of a digital twin, artificial data that mimics actual networks and hosts has been used to assess the prototype.

3.5 Security offence

The significance of cybersecurity in today's constantly linked and digitalized society cannot be emphasized. Organizations that use technology to increase productivity and efficiency are also more vulnerable to a variety of security breaches. Cybersecurity crimes include a variety of malevolent actions, ranging from commonplace dangers like spear phishing to complex cyberattacks like advanced persistent threats (APTs). Gaining an understanding of these offences is essential for creating strong defenses and protecting private data.

The field of cybersecurity is dynamic since hackers are always changing how they take advantage of weaknesses. A wide range of actions intended to jeopardize the availability, confidentiality, or integrity of digital assets are considered security offences. Threat actors' techniques and resources also evolve with technology, therefore a proactive and flexible approach to cybersecurity is required.

To successfully navigate the intricate and ever-changing cybersecurity landscape, security offence plays an essential role. Organizations may successfully reduce risks and maintain resilience against the ever-evolving threat landscape by embracing continuous improvement, integrating offensive plans with strong defense, and taking a proactive approach to risk management. In a digitally linked world, the symbiotic relationship between offence and defense is essential to achieving a comprehensive cybersecurity strategy. Figure 3.2 represents Offensive Cybersecurity framework.

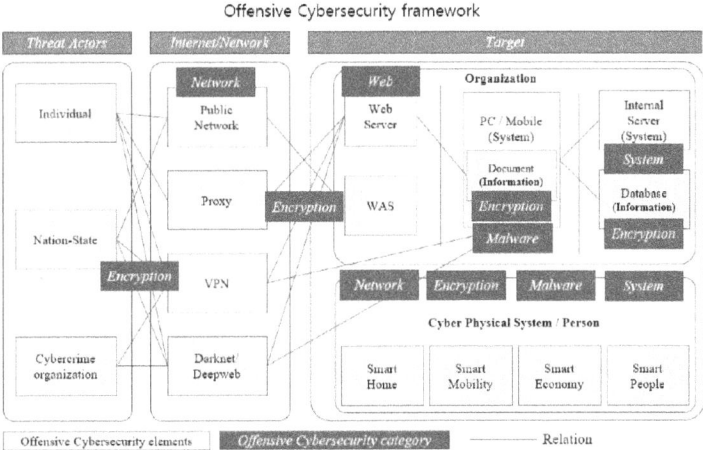

Figure 3.2 Offensive Cybersecurity framework (Kim, Alfouzan, & Kim, Cyber-Attack Scoring Model Based on the Offensive Cybersecurity Framework., 2021).

3.6 Cyber Deception

As a proactive cybersecurity tactic, cyber deception (Pawlick & Zhu, 2021) entails purposefully deceiving adversaries to safeguard networks, systems, and data. One of the most important aspects of cyber deception is drawing in and diverting opponents with the use of decoy devices, such as honeypots. To mislead adversaries and identify their existence, deceptive information, lure operations, and dynamic deception methods are used. The objectives are to improve overall cybersecurity posture, acquire threat intelligence, and lower the likelihood of successful assaults. Cyber deception functions in tandem with other defensive tactics as part of an all-encompassing security plan; it is not a stand-alone solution. Through simulated scenarios, it seeks to hinder attackers, offer early threat detection, and raise user awareness.

The authors (Cranford, et al., 2021) investigate the fundamental cognitive processes involved in making decisions when presented with misleading signals through the lens of this abstract game. A general algorithm that has been used in realistic environments is the SSG. Players pretend to be workers of a corporation, and their objective is to get as many points as possible by "hacking" computers to steal confidential data or keep an eye on them. The defenders must be assigned in the initial step. By calculating the Strong Stackelberg Equilibrium (SSE), which yields each computer's monitoring probability (m-prob) depending on its reward and penalty values, the allocation of the defenders is optimized. Once a computer has been chosen, defenders can use deceptive signaling tactics to their advantage by purposefully giving the attacker information that could be misleading about whether the machine is being watched. After a practice round of five trials, attackers execute four rounds of 25 tries each. Participants are given this information because it is assumed that the agent is perfectly rational and has access to all relevant information at the time of decision-making. Which targets, if chosen, should issue warning signals is decided by the peSSE.

An adaptive cyber deception system is proposed. In a corporate network, ACyDS (Chiang, et al., 2016) gives every server a different virtual network view. A host's perspective on its network, which differs from that of any other host in the network and does not represent actual network configurations, includes subnet topology and IP address assignments of accessible hosts and servers. Every host's network view is dynamically altered by ACyDS, which dynamically creates views with the required attributes. Since subnet topology and

IP address allocations are altered with each view update, ACyDS mandates dynamic network view updates to invalidate intelligence gathered from previous reconnaissance actions.

A concept of hybrid threats and cyber deception is proposed (Steingartner & Galinec, 2021). To provide insights and clarify how to use the model to uncover hidden uncertainties and map disasters to the model, the suggested model expands and changes these categories. Events are categorized by the model based on "identification" and "certainty." A given event's nature is more akin to a fact or piece of knowledge. An event's occurrence may be questionable if its nature is unclear. An unknown unknown is identified, changed from an unknown to a known unknown, and then transferred to this matrix's top right quadrant. Even if we don't know how many uncertainties are still unidentified, turning unknown unknowns into known unknowns entails lowering the total number of unknowns.

The generic deception model (Almeshekah & Spafford, 2016) is the recommendation. Any misleading component goes through three main phases: designing, executing, and integrating, and lastly monitoring and assessing. To successfully plan a deception-based defensive component, there are six key phases. In the second phase of the framework, we need to explain how the attacker, or target, should respond to the deception after defining the strategic goals of the deception process. This deception process's strategic purpose is to lead an attacker to a "fake" account, squandering their resources, and keep an eye on their activities to discover what their goals are.
It is possible to designate a distinct virtual network view for each host or particular host in Usages. This concept (Achleitner, et al., 2016) serves as the foundation for creating and implementing an RDS (Reconnaissance Deception System), which is a formal deception technique. Our deception server, SDN controller, and virtual topology generator work together to create complete network deception while preserving full network functionality for valid traffic. Through the use of malicious scanning techniques on virtual topologies that are emulated in a test environment, we demonstrate that the system may 115 times delay the discovery of susceptible hosts. The controller implementation may detect scanning activity based

on the distribution of network traffic on certain rules by dynamically analyzing SDN flow rule information.

Four teams participated in a real-time red-vs.-blue cyber wargame organized by MITRE (Heckman, et al., 2013): White, Blue CND, Blue Denial & Deception (D&D), and Red. This project offered the chance to combine traditional mission planning and execution—including D&D—with cyber-warfare. The purpose of the cyber-wargame was to evaluate a cyber-security platform for dynamic network defense using the Blackjack CND tool. It also looked into the possibility of enhancing information security in command and control (C2) systems by utilizing D&D. A military scenario created and carried out by Blue utilizing a C2 mission system was used in the cyber-war game. Two hypotheses were tested with this experiment. First, it was thought that Blackjack would effectively prevent adversaries from accessing actual data on the C2 mission system. The second theory held that conventional D&D methods would be successful in keeping the enemy from learning accurate information about the genuine C2 mission system and would instead provide them access to inaccurate information about a fictitious C2 mission system.

The idea offers a two-dimensional framework (Heckman, Stech, Schmoker, & Thomas, 2015) for using D&D methods. Information is related to the first dimension. The second has to do with deeds or customs. The deceiver employs deception to cause misperception by employing the key components of deception information to display what is untrue and uses denial to avoid the discovery of the essential parts of friendly information by hiding what is real. The erroneous information must also be concealed by the deceiver. From a life-cycle viewpoint, the deception chain is a high-level meta-model for cyber D&D operations management. To plan, prepare, and carry out deception operations, the deception chain enables the integration of three systems—cyberD&D, cyber intelligence, and security operations—into the enterprise's wider active defense system. Cyber D&D strategists, cyber-intelligence analysts, and cybersecurity operators are the three equal partners who actively work together to conduct deception operations. The predicted response of the opponent to the deception operation is specified by D&D strategists. D&D planners determine the matching signs that the enemy would see, study the features of the real events and actions that need to be concealed to support the deception cover story, and then devise a strategy to utilize denial The D&D planners and security operations must coordinate and oversee all pertinent preparations if the deception and legitimate operational plans can be synchronized and supported. This will enable them to carry out the deception cover story in a reliable, consistent, and efficient manner. To keep an eye on and manage the deception and actual activities, D&D planners collaborate with cyber intelligence and security operations. The planners could need to carry out a backup deception, go back and review the initial part of the deception chain, or arrange for an alternative operation. tactics to conceal the signatures from the adversary. D&D planners prepare the intended outcome of the deception operation and investigate the tools and resources at their disposal to affect the enemy.

3.7 Malware Detection

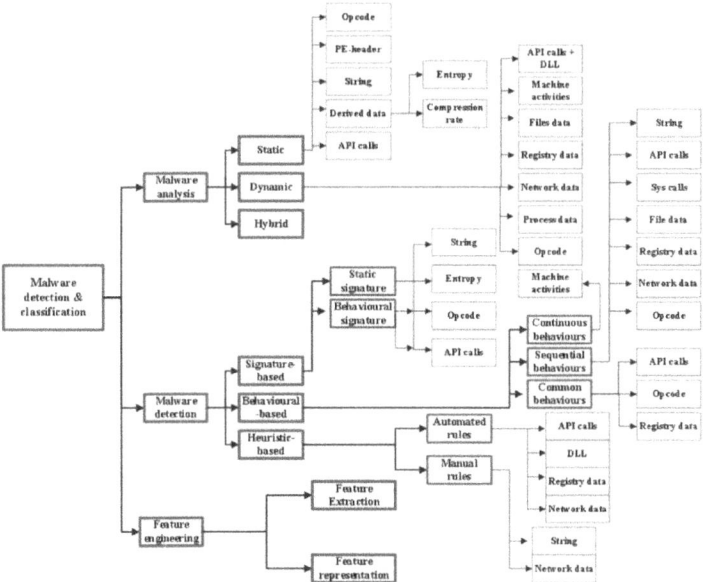

Figure 3.3 Malware analysis and detection Taxonomy (Aboaoja, et al., 2022).

The persistent danger provided by malicious software, or malware (He, et al., 2021), is one of the most important concerns in the intricate and constantly changing field of cybersecurity. Malware may take many different forms, ranging from common viruses and worms to more advanced ransomware and spyware. One of the most important aspects of protecting networks, computer systems, and sensitive data is identifying and eliminating these threats. A vast array of harmful software is referred to as malware, and its purpose is to jeopardize the availability, confidentiality, or integrity of digital assets. A few instances are trojans, which pose as trustworthy software, viruses, which multiply and propagate across a host system, and ransomware, which encrypts data to demand ransom. A successful malware assault can have serious repercussions, including financial losses, data leaks, and interruptions to vital infrastructure. To stop these attacks from wreaking havoc on an organization's digital ecology, malware detection is essential. Figure 3.3 represents Malware analysis and detection Taxonomy. Figure 3.4 represents Taxonomy of Malware analysis.

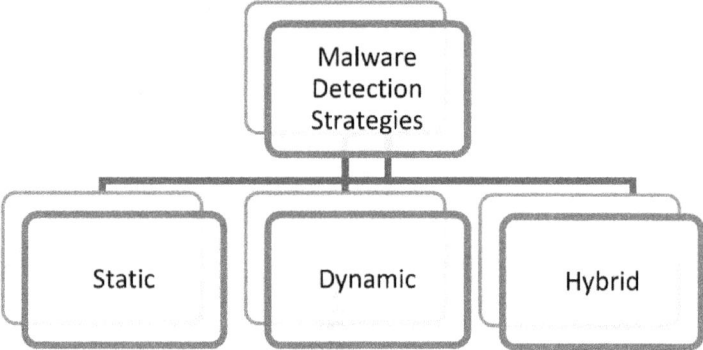

Figure 3.4 Taxonomy of Malware analysis (Tayyab, Khan, Durad, Khan, & Lee, 2022).

Figure 3.5 Different types of Malware attacks (Akhtar & Feng, Detection of Malware by Deep Learning as CNN-LSTM Machine Learning Techniques in Real Time., 2022).

The kernel extreme learning machine (KELM), regularised random vector functional link neural network (RRVFLN), and least square support vector machine (LS-SVM) are the three machine learning models used in the ensemble learning process of the AAMD-OELAC approach (Alamro, et al., 2023). Data preparation is done in the beginning to enhance the quality of the real data. All Android applications can remove both permissions and API calls, which are database features. Androguard is the name of a comprehensive package utility designed only for Python platforms and intended to deal with Android files. It could be used as a tool for Android application reverse engineering. By deleting the DEX file permissions from each APK file separately, the Androguard program may be used to analyze APK files.

The suggested application is Transformers' design for automated malware detection (Rahali & Akhloufi, 2021). This model, which is based on BERT (Bidirectional Encoder Representations from Transformers), uses preprocessed features to perform a static analysis on the source code of Android applications to characterize and categorize malware that has already been discovered into several representative groups. It uses text preprocessing on these features to preserve pertinent data, such as actions, intentions, and permissions. The Android apps were gathered from the Androzoo public dataset.

There are presently 13,320,014 distinct APKs on there, and hundreds of antivirus programs have examined each one to determine which apps are flagged as malicious. It used Jdax, which generates folders containing the app files, to decompile the downloaded APKs. From every sample, the AndroidManifest.xml file was extracted. The manifest provides the Android system with important details about the application, details the system needs to know before it can execute any of the application's code. These details include the version number, the activities, services, broadcast receivers, content providers, list of permissions, and meta-data. The cleaning process involved removing vocabulary and punctuation while preserving the character cases and numbers. The final dataset format consists of four columns: a binary format for the Label column, the Text column (which represents the Manifest files after preprocessing), the APK hash name for the ID column, and so on.

The executable (Kancherla & Mukkamala, 2013) is first transformed from binary to an 8-bit, one-dimensional vector. The pixel's intensity is then calculated from the 8-bit value. In the end, we transform the one-dimensional vector into a two-dimensional one. Depending on the file size, the image's width is fixed. Subsequently, we extract characteristics derived from images, such as those based on intensity, wavelet, and Gabor. In our tests, it employed 15,000 malware samples and 12,000 benign samples. Windows XP, Windows Vista, Windows 7, and Windows NT are the sources of benign samples. The 534 features in the dataset are divided into 512 Gabor-based features, 16 Wavelet-based features, and 6 intensity-based features.

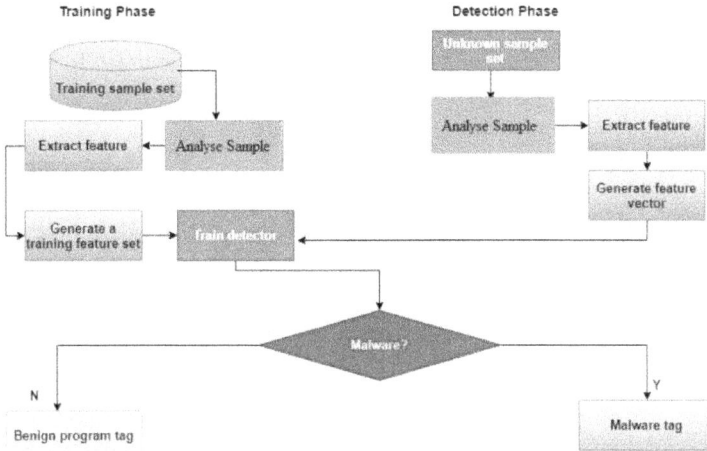

Figure 3.6 Proposed ML malware detection method (Akhtar & Feng, Malware Analysis and Detection Using Machine Learning Algorithms, 2022).

The article (Akhtar & Feng, Malware Analysis and Detection Using Machine Learning Algorithms, 2022) describes the different phases and elements of a standard machine learning workflow for malware detection and classification, examines its drawbacks and restrictions, and evaluates the most recent advancements and trends in the industry, with a focus on deep learning methods. Numerous data files in the collection include log data for different kinds of malware. Numerous models may be trained using these recovered log characteristics. The files themselves were unprocessed executables, and the data were saved in the file system as binary code. It constructed a smaller collection of features from a bigger set; this method is frequently employed to use fewer features and still retain the same level of accuracy. Feature selection was carried out following feature extraction, which required finding more features. Figure 3.6 represents the same.

3.8 Forensic Analysis

Digital evidence, including files, network traffic, and logs, are systematically examined in forensic analysis to recreate events, find security flaws, and assign actions to particular people or entities. In cybersecurity, forensic analysis is an essential field that focuses on looking into and evaluating digital occurrences to find information, comprehend the nature of risks, and assist with legal proceedings.

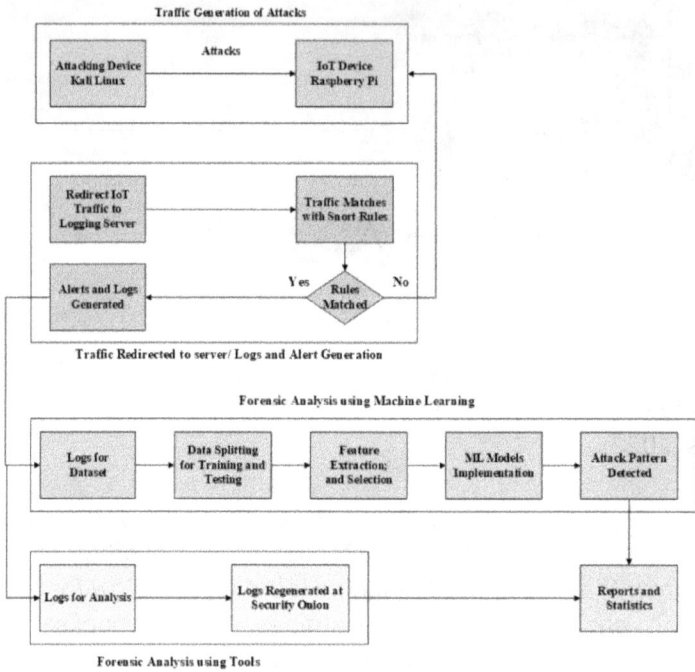

Figure 3.7 Proposed methodology (Mazhar, et al., 2022).

There are four elements in the suggested framework (Mazhar, et al., 2022) for forensic investigation of compromised IoT devices. Initially, assaults are generated via traffic from the Kali Linux system to the IoT devices that are being utilized for testing. Second, traffic from IoT devices is sent to a logging server, where it is analyzed and logs and alerts are created when the traffic matches rules stored in the logging server. This process is handled by the traffic redirection logging server and alerts/logs generation. Third, the regeneration of the logs that the logging server has acquired is the responsibility of forensic analysis utilizing a forensic server. The required data on the attack and the attacker is collected from the regenerated logs. Fourth, by employing various machine learning models, forensic analysis employing machine learning is in charge of identifying assaults. Figure 3.7 represents the same.

The recommendation (Shahbazi & Byun, 2022) strengthens the DF analysis's security concerning data posted on social media. The processing layer, interface layer, analysis layer, data layer, and knowledge layer are the five key layers of this process. The processing layer is in charge of locating and obtaining system input. Social media networks and incident notifications provide inputs, and to identify them, the event description and incident boundary definition are needed. Before acquiring, the identification, extraction, data collecting, parsing, and preservation are necessary. The forensic data is the data layer's input, completing this procedure. This layer stores the data and uses a hybrid data mapping for both local and global ontologies. The next layer is the analysis layer, where correlation events and document analysis, location analysis, relatedness of results, frequency analysis, and connection analysis are the analysis operators, and the interface question is an NLP semantic interface. The temporal graph, location chart, frequency chart, timelines, tweet cloud, interaction graph, and interaction graph are all included in the interface layer of the analysis report. The relationship between the extracted dataset and its linkage is handled in the knowledge layer, which comes next. The examined dataset is prepared for saving into the blockchain framework following the completion of the NLP procedures and data processing.

The data collecting tasks at two different cyber security exercises (McClain, et al., 2015). Behavioral performance based on human-machine interactions and questionnaire-based evaluations of cyber security expertise were two of the many methods used in this data gathering. The subjects were 26 individuals all of whom gave their permission for data gathering to be collected during two different cyber security training exercises called Tracer FIRE. In the first section, participants were asked to rate, on a six-point scale, their professional and academic experiences with six different kinds of cyber security forensics investigation. The Tracer FIRE exercises were multi-day events that included a team competition exercise together with classroom instruction on the use of forensic analysis methodologies, adversary tactics, and cyber security software tools. A statement about the study was made at the start of the competition, and participants who agreed to participate in the data-gathering procedure completed the informed consent form. Over the course of the multi-day activity, questionnaire assessments were given out. Automated data logging was used to capture non-intrusive data on human-machine exchanges as the individuals completed the activity.

References

Aboaoja, F., Zainal, A., Ghaleb, F., Al-rimy, B., Eisa, T., & Elnour, A. (2022). Malware Detection Issues, Challenges, and Future Directions: A Survey. *Applied Sciences., 12*(17), 8482.

Achleitner, S., La Porta, T., M. P., Sugrim, S., Krishnamurthy, S. V., & Chadha, R. (2016). Cyber deception: Virtual networks to defend insider reconnaissance. *8th ACM CCS international workshop on managing insider security threats* (pp. 57-68). Vienna Austria: ACM.

Akhtar, M., & Feng, T. (2022). Detection of Malware by Deep Learning as CNN-LSTM Machine Learning Techniques in Real Time. *Symmetry, 14*(11), 2308.

Akhtar, M., & Feng, T. (2022). Malware Analysis and Detection Using Machine Learning Algorithms. *Symmetry, 14*(11), 2304.

Alamro, H., Mtouaa, W., Aljameel, S., Salama, A. S., Hamza, M. A., & Othman, A. Y. (2023). Automated android malware detection using optimal ensemble learning approach for cybersecurity. *IEEE Access.*

Albasheer, H., Md Siraj, M., Mubarakali, A., Elsier Tayfour, O., Salih, S., Hamdan, M., . . . Kamarudeen, S. (2022). Cyber-Attack Prediction Based on Network Intrusion Detection Systems for Alert Correlation Techniques: A Survey. *Sensors, 22*(4), 1494.

Almeshekah, M. H., & Spafford, E. H. (2016). Cyber security deception. . *Cyber Deception: Building the Scientific Foundation*, 23-50.

Alserhani, F., Akhlaq, M., Awan, I. U., & Cullen, A. J. (2010). Detection of coordinated attacks using alert correlation model. *IEEE International Conference on Progress in Informatics and Computing. 1*, pp. 542-546. Shanghai, China: IEEE.

Ambika, N. (2020). Improved Methodology to Detect Advanced Persistent Threat Attacks. In N. K. Chaubey, & B. B. Prajapati, *Quantum Cryptography and the Future of Cyber Security* (pp. 184-202). US: IGI Global.

Ambika, N. (2022). Minimum Prediction Error at an Early Stage in Darknet Analysis. In *Dark Web Pattern Recognition and Crime Analysis Using Machine Intelligence* (pp. 18-30). US: IGI Global.

Ambika, N. (2022). Precise Risk Assessment and Management. In *Cyber-Physical Systems: Foundations and Techniques* (pp. 63-83). Canada.: Wiley.

Chiang, C., Gottlieb, Y., Sugrim, S., Chadha, R., Serban, C., Poylisher, A., . . . Santos, J. (2016). ACyDS: An adaptive cyber deception system. *IEEE Military Communications Conference* (pp. 800-805). Baltimore, MD, USA: IEEE.

Cranford, E. A., Gonzalez, C., Aggarwal, P., Tambe, M., Cooney, S., & Lebiere, C. (2021). Towards a cognitive theory of cyber deception. *Cognitive Science, 45*(7), e13013.

Gao, P., Shao, F., Liu, X., Xiao, X., Qin, Z., Xu, F., . . . Song, D. (2021). Enabling efficient cyber threat hunting with cyber threat intelligence. *37th International Conference on Data Engineering (ICDE)* (pp. 193-204). Chania, Greece: IEEE.

Granadillo, G. G., El-Barbori, M., & Debar, H. (2016). New types of alert correlation for security information and event management systems. . *8th IFIP international conference on new technologies, mobility and security (NTMS)* (pp. 1-7). Larnaca, Cyprus: IEEE.

He, Z., Miari, T., Makrani, H. M., Aliasgari, M., Homayoun, H., & Sayadi, H. (2021). When machine learning meets hardware cybersecurity: Delving into accurate zero-day malware detection. *22nd International Symposium on Quality Electronic Design (ISQED)* (pp. 85-90). Santa Clara, CA, USA: IEEE.

Heckman, K. E., Stech, F. J., Schmoker, B. S., & Thomas, R. K. (2015). Denial and deception in cyber defense. *Computer, 48*(4), 36-44.

Heckman, K. E., Walsh, M. J., Stech, F. J., O'boyle, T. A., DiCato, S. R., & Herber, A. F. (2013). Active cyber defense with denial and deception: A cyber-wargame experiment. *computers & security, 37*, 72-77.

Jadidi, Z., & Lu, Y. (2021). A threat hunting framework for industrial control systems. *IEEE Access, 9*, 164118-164130.

Kancherla, K., & Mukkamala, S. (2013). Image visualization based malware detection. *IEEE Symposium on Computational Intelligence in Cyber Security (CICS)* (pp. 40-44). Singapore: IEEE.

Khosravi, M., & Ladani, B. T. (2020). Alerts correlation and causal analysis for APT based cyber attack detection. *IEEE Access, 8*, 162642-162656.

Kim, K., Alfouzan, F., & Kim, H. (2021). Cyber-Attack Scoring Model Based on the Offensive Cybersecurity Framework. *Applied Sciences., 11*(16), 7738.

Kim, K., Alshenaifi, I., Ramachandran, S., Kim, J., Zia, T., & Almorjan, A. (2023). Cybersecurity and Cyber Forensics for Smart Cities: A Comprehensive Literature Review and Survey. *Sensors, 23*(7), 3681.

Lozano, M. A., Llopis, I. P., & Domingo, M. E. (2023). Threat Hunting Architecture Using a Machine Learning Approach for Critical Infrastructures Protection. *Big Data and Cognitive Computing, 7*(2), 65.

Mavroeidis, V., & Jøsang, A. (2018). Data-driven threat hunting using sysmon. *2nd international conference on cryptography, security and privacy* (pp. 82-88). Guiyang China: ACM.

Mazhar, M., Saleem, Y., Almogren, A., Arshad, J., Jaffery, M., Rehman, A., . . . Hamam, H. (2022). Forensic Analysis on Internet of Things (IoT) Device Using Machine-to-Machine (M2M) Framework. *Electronics, 11*(7), 1126.

McClain, J., Silva, A., Emmanuel, G., Anderson, B., Nauer, K. A., & Forsythe, C. (2015). Human performance factors in cyber security forensic analysis. . *6th International Conference on Applied Human Factors and Ergonomics (AHFE 2015)* (pp. 5301-5307). Caesars Palace, Las Vegas, USA: ELSEVIER.

Miazi, M. N., Pritom, M. M., Shehab, M., Chu, B., & Wei, J. (2017). The design of cyber threat hunting games: A case study. . *26th International Conference on Computer Communication and Networks (ICCCN)* (pp. 1-6). Vancouver, BC, Canada: IEEE.

Neto, A. J., & dos Santos, A. F. (2020). Cyber threat hunting through automated hypothesis and multi-criteria decision making. *International Conference on Big Data (Big Data)* (pp. 1823-1830). Atlanta, GA, USA: IEEE.

Pawlick, J., & Zhu, Q. (2021). *Game theory for cyber deception.* CHAM: Springer International Publishing.

Pontes, E., Guelfi, A. E., Kofuji, S. T., & Silva, A. A. (2011). Applying multi-correlation for improving forecasting in cyber security. *Sixth International Conference on Digital Information Management* (pp. 179-186). Melbourne, VIC, Australia: IEEE.

Rahali, A., & Akhloufi, M. A. (2021). *MalBERT: Using transformers for cybersecurity and malicious software detection.* Newyork: cornell university.

Shahbazi, Z., & Byun, Y.-C. (2022). NLP-Based Digital Forensic Analysis for Online Social Network Based on System Security. *International Journal of Environmental Research and Public Health, 19*(12), 7027.

Shittu, R., Healing, A., Ghanea-Hercock, R., Bloomfield, R., & Rajarajan, M. (2015). Intrusion alert prioritisation and attack detection using post-correlation analysis. *Computers & Security, 50*, 1-15.

Singer, P. W., & Friedman, A. (2014). *Cybersecurity: What everyone needs to know*. University of Oxford: oup usa.

Sree, V. S., Koganti, C. S., Kalyana, S. K., & Anudeep, P. (2021). Artificial intelligence based predictive threat hunting in the field of cyber security. . *2nd Global Conference for Advancement in Technology (GCAT)* (pp. 1-6). Bangalore, India: IEEE.

Steingartner, W., & Galinec, D. (2021). Cyber threats and cyber deception in hybrid warfare. *Acta Polytechnica Hungarica, 18*(3), 25-45.

Tayyab, U.-e.-H., Khan, F., Durad, M., Khan, A., & Lee, Y. (2022). A Survey of the Recent Trends in Deep Learning Based Malware Detection. *Journal of Cybersecurity and Privacy, 2*(4), 800-829.

Wu, M., & Moon, Y. (2019). Alert correlation for cyber-manufacturing intrusion detection. *47th SME North American Manufacturing Research Conference. 34*, pp. 820-831. Pennsylvania, USA.: ELSEVIER.

Zhang, K., Zhao, F., Luo, S., Xin, Y., & Zhu, H. (2019). An intrusion action-based IDS alert correlation analysis and prediction framework. *IEEE Access, 7*, 150540-150551.

CHAPTER 4

SECURITY MEASURES

Abstract

The significance of cybersecurity in the quickly evolving digital world, when technology touches every aspect of our lives, cannot be emphasized. The world of computers, which includes networks, systems, and data, is always facing new risks, which might range from deliberate assaults to unintentional weaknesses. Strong defenses against unwanted access, data breaches, and disruptive cyber disasters are becoming more and more necessary as our dependence on linked technology grows.

The field of cybersecurity is devoted to protecting digital assets and guaranteeing information availability, confidentiality, and integrity in the face of changing threats. The world of cyberspace is constantly changing, as hackers and cybercriminals use advanced methods to take advantage of holes in networks and systems. To safeguard sensitive data and vital infrastructure, people, organizations, and governments must take a proactive and all-encompassing strategy.

Keywords: Cybercrime, cyber attack

4.1 Introduction

Cybersecurity is an important and ever-evolving discipline that focuses on defending systems, data, and digital assets from many types of attacks. In today's technologically advanced and networked world, cybersecurity is essential to protecting people, businesses, and governments against harmful activity.

4.2 Cyber Resilience Lifecycle

Proactive steps, such as risk assessment and mitigation plans, are taken from the start of the lifecycle to make sure that organizations are ready for any risks. The reaction phase has essential importance in the case of a cyber disaster, necessitating prompt and efficient efforts to minimize damage and expedite recovery. The lessons learned are integrated into an adaptive feedback loop after the event, which promotes continuous development and increases resilience all around. Figure 4.1 represents the Cyber Resilience lifecycle.

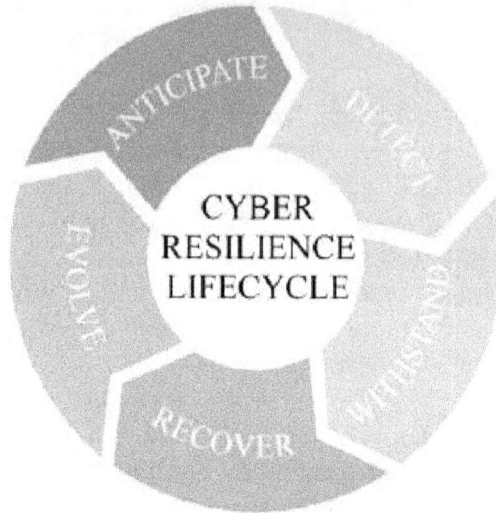

Figure 4.1 Cyber Resilience lifecycle (Vogel, Dyka, Klann, & Langendörfer, 2021).

4.2.1 Anticipate

A strategy approach called cyber resilience (Petrenko, 2022) anticipation aims to improve an organization's capacity to foresee, endure, recover from, and adapt to cyberattacks. Businesses and individuals are continually exposed to a wide range of cyber dangers in today's linked and digital society. These risks can range from sophisticated cyberattacks to unanticipated weaknesses. Anticipating cyber resilience (Ligo, Kott, & Linkov, 2021) involves more than just standard cybersecurity measures; it involves proactive approaches to foresee, anticipate, and lessen the effects of possible threats.

Semi-structured interviews (Carías, Arrizabalaga, Labaka, & Hernantes, 2020) were employed in this study as a qualitative data source to create a cyber resilience progression model. Semi-structured interviews are a valuable method of data gathering for qualitative research that allows for the collection of personal experiences related to a certain topic or area. Because of their extensive knowledge in the field, the experts were picked, and their profiles were chosen to complement the three viewpoints on the subject. These three viewpoints were thought to add value to the study because academics are rigorous but frequently cut off from practitioners' empirical experience; practitioners in organizations frequently have this experience but may not always be up to date on the latest developments in the field; and cybersecurity providers are committed to putting cyber resilience policies into place in businesses daily, so they may have some combination of the other two perspectives. The variety of backgrounds further supported the use of semi-structured interviews as a means of guaranteeing a consistent comprehension of the interview's questions and language.

Eleven major players were interviewed in-depth and semi-structured (Groenendaal & Helsloot, 2021). According to the interviews, the company operated cyber resiliently in that the amount of occurrences and their effects did not increase noticeably. According to the interviews, all four resilience skills were technically created before the COVID-19 pandemic, but they hardly ever led to anticipatory adjustment. According to the interviews, the organization's cyber resilience during the pandemic crisis was mostly attributed to its capacity for response. From the interviews, three conclusions concerning the GFI's handling of the difficulties brought on by the COVID-19 pandemic problem can be made.

The framework (van der Kleij & Leukfeldt, 2020) guarantees the viability of human components of cyber security that are essential to an organization's business continuity, while also giving them diagnostic capabilities to better prepare for future cyber threats. A conceptual framework of resilient behavior is produced by combining the three sources of behavior and the four resilience functions. The Cyber Resilient Behaviour Questionnaire was first developed and then improved based on input from experts and a small sample of SMEs to ensure the survey's validity. 42 statements total on the updated instrument's six-point Likert-type scale, which lacks a midpoint.

4.2.2 Detect

A thorough cybersecurity plan must include cyber resilience detection, which focuses on the early detection and mitigation of possible attacks. This strategy emphasizes threat intelligence analysis, scenario preparation, and ongoing monitoring, going above and beyond standard security precautions. Using threat intelligence, carrying out routine risk assessments, creating scenarios, and placing a high priority on staff awareness and training are important elements. Early threat detection, decreased downtime, improved recovery capabilities, and flexibility to new threats are all advantages of cyber resilience detection. In the end, businesses that put a high priority on cyber resilience detection are better positioned to foresee, fend off, and recover from cyber assaults in our increasingly linked digital environment.

Various AI models, algorithms, and technologies used in threat identification, response, and recovery procedures are evaluated in this study (Vegesna, 2023). Additionally, it evaluates how well AI-integrated systems respond to changing cyber threats, highlighting their contribution to bolstering networks' and organizations' security posture. A multimodal method is used to collect data, drawing from a variety of sources including cybersecurity event reports, case studies, and conversations with AI-driven cybersecurity solution vendors. Examining different AI models, algorithms, and technologies used in cybersecurity is the assessment step. Thematic analysis and coding approaches are used to thoroughly analyze qualitative data gathered from focus groups, interviews, and conversations to find recurrent themes and topics that are emerging. There are steps made to ensure that participants give their informed permission and that data processing and reporting adhere to ethical norms. The research findings are considered to provide significant findings regarding the influence of AI on cybersecurity resilience, along with practical suggestions and future research paths.

The outcomes of a weighted outlier analysis can be used to create a cyber-attack matrix (CAM) (Hopkins, Kalaimannan, & John, 2020). The CAM forecasts a data point's leverage, influence, and outlier qualities. Data may be categorized as excellent, poor, or attacked using the CAM as a decision-making tool. Cyber-attack data categorization will be incorporated into the revised version of the traditional state estimate procedure. A predict phase, a phase for classifying cyberattack data, a phase for predicting without cyberattack data, and an update phase comprise the new procedure. Estimator analysis, data characterization, Cyber Attack Matrix building, and state estimation process update development are some of the techniques used in this study. The study will assess the effectiveness of various estimators and identify benefits for CPS combining IT and OT devices.

4.2.3 Withstand

The danger landscape for organizations has changed in a more digital and linked world, making cybersecurity a crucial component of corporate operations. A systematic method known as "cyber resilience" is developed to protect against cyber threats and guarantee business continuity in the event of unavoidable cyber catastrophes. Cyber resilience, in contrast to traditional methods that only concentrate on prevention, recognizes that security breaches are a question of "when," not "if."

4.2.4 Recover

Recognizing that cyber threats are not only persistent but also constantly changing is the first step toward building cyber resilience. To stay one step ahead of cyber attackers, organizations need to plan and adjust their strategy to account for anticipated threats. Given how much technology is used by organizations in today's digital world, cyber-attacks are inevitable and need a deliberate and flexible response. A complete architecture known as "cyber resilience" includes both preventive steps to avert cyber catastrophes and effective recovery plans for when an attack occurs. This dual focus on recovery and resilience recognizes that cyber-attacks are dynamic and that organizations must recover quickly and safely.

Compared to the NIST CSF, the work (Onwubiko, 2020) has 42 subcomponents and 8 key components: identify, control, map, plan, playbook, measure, test, and improve. There are just three main recovery categories and six subcategories. The first essential element of the framework is identification. It focuses on identifying an organization's most important technical and non-technical assets, which need to be promptly restored in the case of a major cyber catastrophe, data breach, or cyber attack. The second essential element of the structure is control. Its main goal is to assist the organization in understanding what cyber recovery controls it has and how much they may aid in the organization's ability to recover from a cyberattack. To prioritize assets, one of Map's primary components is to map important assets to their dependencies and organizational importance. It also outlines the steps involved in recovery and restoration in the case of a cyber incident. The main goal of this framework component is to develop a recovery objective plan, processes, and procedures. It also outlines the stakeholders and their roles and duties, outlining who should be notified in the case of a cyber incident for recovery. A playbook is a comprehensive record of all the "What If" and cyber wargaming scenarios that must be run beforehand to be ready for the various kinds of cyberattacks, as well as the recovery techniques that need to be used to get services back up and running. It also includes any backup plans that might be used to either operate the service in a less-than-ideal state until full recovery and restoration are finished, or backout procedures that should be used and by whom. To determine whether restoration and recovery have been successful or not, measures such as service and operational level agreements, key performance indicators, and recovery objectives are defined. This information is then used to inform future adjustments to the service or the recovery approach, controls, and capabilities. A variety of tests must be performed to make sure that recovery capabilities are suitable and that recovery controls are working. It is advised that recovery testing be a constant endeavor. The final element of the framework, "improve," highlights the necessity of ongoing development, lessons learned, adaptability, training, and skill advancement.

4.2.5 Evolve

In a time of digital revolution, technological advancement has brought with it previously unheard-of benefits as well as difficulties. Today's digital environment is linked, which has led to the emergence of several cyber threats, from sophisticated malware to intricate social engineering techniques. The notion of cyber resilience has become essential in an ever-changing landscape for enterprises that aim to protect themselves against cyberattacks while simultaneously being able to adjust, bounce back, and prosper in the face of unavoidable setbacks.

Cyber resilience is a comprehensive approach that recognizes the inevitable nature of cyberattacks and gives equal weight to planning, response, and recovery, going beyond the traditional approach that concentrates only on prevention. Organizations must modify their cyber resilience plans in response to new threats as they arise to successfully address them.

This growth necessitates a proactive and all-encompassing strategy that includes ongoing evaluation, adaptable security measures, teamwork, and a dedication to taking lessons from both achievements and setbacks. Shaped by strategic alliances, staff training, and the integration of state-of-the-art technology, a robust cybersecurity posture is essential.

4.3 Different types of Cyber security

Technology is evolving at a rate that has never before allowed for such extraordinary conveniences and opportunities in our digitally linked society. But there are also a lot of difficulties associated with this interconnection, especially when it comes to protecting digital assets and private data from bad actors. Cybersecurity has become a critical activity, safeguarding computer systems, networks, and data from damage, threats, and unauthorized access.

As the digital realm grows, cybersecurity's reach also broadens. Numerous cybersecurity techniques have surfaced, each specifically designed to tackle distinct aspects of the intricate problems presented by cyber attacks. Cybersecurity has developed into a broad field that includes protecting data, adopting new technologies like the Internet of Things (IoT), and securing networks and endpoints.

This investigation attempts to provide and delve into many forms of cybersecurity, illuminating the distinct tactics and technology used to strengthen the digital domain. Every aspect of cybersecurity, whether it is centered on the protection of specific devices, programs, or the larger network architecture, is essential to building a strong defense against online attacks.

4.3.1 Information security

Information availability, confidentiality, and integrity are the three main areas of focus for information security, a subset of cybersecurity. It includes not just digital data but also the procedures, guidelines, and standards that control its entire existence. The goal of information security is to establish a safe environment where data is protected against unwanted access, modification, or deletion. To reduce hazards, this all-encompassing strategy applies strong access restrictions, encryption techniques, and close monitoring.

The growing dependence of both individuals and organizations on digital platforms for communication, collaboration, and storage highlights the critical relationship between information security and cybersecurity. The modern technological landscape is so linked that it necessitates a unified approach to security that takes into account human variables as well as technical ones, such as user awareness and policy compliance.

This investigation seeks to dissect the layers of security required to safely traverse the digital terrain by delving into the complexities of cybersecurity and information security. Navigating these security domains requires constant resilience and adaptation in the face of new threats, from learning the subtleties of network defenses to putting encryption mechanisms that protect critical data into place.

To gather information from websites about privacy, the work designates two input templates that serve as search engine query questions. Investigating the extent of privacy universality is the first step. The quantity of web pages about a certain privacy measure indicates how widely applicable it is. Counting the number of web pages about privacy and secrecy is the second stage. Users' worries with privacy disclosure are represented in the inquiries that pertain to privacy confidentiality. The work (Lu, Qu, Li, & Hui, 2015) is a privacy information security classification (PISC) model for privacy in the Internet of Things (IoT) and CPS. According to this model, the security level of the privacy information is based on the outcome of the privacy disclosure, which takes into account two factors: the number of parties participating in the privacy and the extent of the disclosure. High security, medium security, basic security, and poor security are the four security tiers.

Using survey data from 192 visitors of a newly hijacked website, the concept is empirically evaluated (Lee & Lee, 2012). It uses statistical analysis and a web-based questionnaire survey approach. Real data was gathered in June 2008 by a significant Korean market research firm. First, the writers conducted an exploratory analysis of the retreative behaviors of online buyers. Auction participants' retreating behavior-related responses were analyzed both inside the group and in contrast to non-members' actions. The information security event can have a quantifiable detrimental effect on consumer behavior, according to the data analysis results, even if the effect appears to be mostly confined to that one website. According to the tested model of retreating behaviors, victims' perceived harm and the availability of alternative shopping sources can greatly increase their retreating behaviors. On the other hand, victims' perceptions of the website's relative usefulness and ease of use have little effect on their retreating behavior.

4.3.2 Network Security

Within the larger topic of cybersecurity (Ambika N. , 2021), network security (Ahuja, 1996) (Stallings, 1995)is a discipline that focuses on protecting the confidentiality and integrity of data as it moves across computer networks. It includes a wide range of tools, procedures, and guidelines made to shield networks from intrusions, online dangers, and data leaks. The goal is to protect the underlying infrastructure, which consists of servers, routers, switches, and other network components, in addition to securing the data while it is in transit.

The environment of the cyber world is one of ongoing innovation and changing dangers. Network security must be one step ahead of those looking to take advantage of vulnerabilities for nefarious ends, given the surge in sophisticated cyberattacks and the expansion of Internet of Things (IoT) (Ambika N. , 2020) units.

4.3.3 Operational Security

A key component of cybersecurity is operational security, which is a methodical approach created to recognize, manage, and safeguard critical data and activities. OPSEC employs a comprehensive strategy that takes into account people, procedures, and physical security in addition to technology. Its objective is to stop adversaries from obtaining data that they may use to take advantage of weaknesses, jeopardize assets, or jeopardize an entity's ability to operate.

By navigating the nexus between operational security and the cyber world, this investigation reveals the tactics and methods necessary to sustain a safe and reliable operating environment. Operating security is a constant struggle to keep ahead of changing threats, from encrypting sensitive data to putting in place access restrictions that prevent unwanted access.

A model (Haddad, et al., 2011) is made up of Derived Measures (DMs), which are subsequently put together in assurance metrics, based on the interpretation of Base Measures (BMs), or system raw data. Since the BMs that could become accessible in the future for generic models are unknown, only abstract metrics and DMs can be provided. The known risks and SOs for the service and the system delivering it establish the security measures that need to be reviewed. An AMO is defined as a high-level metric proving that the SR is satisfied for each of its associated (abstract) IOs. One or more AMRs are then created from each AMO, measuring the various dimensions of the related (abstract) IOs. The additional OSA-AF entities are installed and operational, as are the necessary system probes. The presentation process entails giving the users pertinent system views together with the security assurance evaluation results.

4.3.4 Internet Security

The proactive defense system used to safeguard the extensive and linked network of computers, apps, and data that travels over the Internet is known as Internet security. It covers a wide variety of threats, including malware, phishing, cyberattacks, and other criminal actions that jeopardize the availability, confidentiality, and integrity of digital assets.

This investigation explores the crucial nexus between Internet security and the cyber world, revealing the security layers necessary to provide a secure and safe online experience. Internet security is a diverse strategy for risk mitigation and reinforcing the digital infrastructure, ranging from the deployment of firewalls and intrusion detection systems to the application of encryption algorithms to safeguard data in transit.

4.4 End-user Education

An essential part of cybersecurity is end-user education, which aims to provide people in an organization with the knowledge and skills they need to make decisions that are both secure and well-informed. Human factors are important in the constantly changing world of cyber threats, and end-user education contributes to the development of a strong defense against cyberattacks.

End-user education, often referred to as cybersecurity training or user awareness training, gives people the information, abilities, and awareness needed to identify and react to any cybersecurity threats. Employees, contractors, and everyone else who uses the digital systems and data of an organization are all covered by this education.

The National Initiative for Cybersecurity Education (NICE) Framework (AlDaajeh, et al., 2022) is used in the proposal to link cybersecurity strategic goals to cybersecurity skills and capabilities. The learning outcomes for the recently proposed cybersecurity education and training programs' curricula were developed using the GQO+ Strategies paradigm and based on the three main strategic goals of cybersecurity: defending against sophisticated cyber threats, developing secure digital and information technology infrastructure and services, and enhancing cybersecurity awareness and maturity among individuals. NICE functions as a vocabulary and reference structure. To increase the capabilities of their workforce in cybersecurity work, it helps organizations and sectors create a uniform and consistent vocabulary and categories for cybersecurity job skills, knowledge, and competencies. It benefits students on two levels: professionally and in terms of awareness.

4.5 Use Cases

At the federal government level in the United States, case studies (Chatfield & Reddick, 2019) are conducted to examine digital technology policy, IoT cybersecurity policy, and IoT adoption in key application fields. According to the framework, the development and utilization of IoT-enabled dynamic capabilities will play a major role in driving and expediting the digital transformation of public administration and governance, ultimately leading to smart government performance outcomes. The approach also assumes that creating and executing two complementary and successful public policy strands would have an impact on the IoT-enabled dynamic capabilities. To gather more than thirty government papers on IoT technology assessments, IoT use cases, and IoT cybersecurity regulations, it looked through the websites of federal government agencies. The case study materials were then evaluated.

To train users and students to conduct these audits and then strengthen the security of the identified vulnerable IoT devices, a use case-based approach (Fernández-Caramés & Fraga-Lamas, 2020) is put out. Students will get a list of Shodan searches from the teacher. The students identify the IoT device they are seeking and its intended usage by analyzing the results of each inquiry. Typically, this procedure entails conducting many Google searches to locate vendor materials such as device manuals or datasheets. Studying the vulnerabilities found by Shodan, the students search for default credentials and other possible cybersecurity issues.

This article's work (Jofre, et al., 2021) was developed as a component of the Secure and Private Health Data Exchange (CUREX) initiative of the European Union (EU). The CUREX solution computes cybersecurity and privacy risk ratings related to data sharing in a health domain by analyzing data from the monitoring infrastructure. There are five distinct sections in CUREX. Finding assets and vulnerabilities find out what the system's resources are and any information about any vulnerabilities they may have. Threat intelligence is the process of identifying novel and unidentified threats by identifying abnormalities in data as well as odd behaviors on users' devices in real-time. risk management creating risk scores and ideal defences for the healthcare organization's cyber-strategy. Increasing trust, private and sensitive data may be shared and stored on a decentralized blockchain network. Three possibilities are outlined in this paper. To assess the course of the use case, "network configuration" poses no cybersecurity or privacy risks. "Outpatient appointment check" poses a risk of misuse because a denial-of-service attack could prevent legitimate users from accessing internet services, including outpatient information for patients. "Visualisation of clinical information" poses a risk of misuse because it suggests using an inside URL attack to retrieve clinical information, which also poses a privacy.

The paper (Fernández-Caramés & Fraga-Lamas, 2020) describes how IIoT and Industry 4.0 cybersecurity can be taught through real-world use cases, utilizing a methodology that enables audits to be conducted with students who have no prior knowledge of IIoT or industrial cybersecurity. The authors have taught 119 students an IIoT and Industry 4.0 course in the past several years using the approach and materials outlined in this article. The lecturer gave each student three distinct Shodan searches to research before assigning them to automate the search using Python scripts.

There is a malware signature available that causes the system to suffer serious harm. The anti-malware program is unable to identify the ongoing harmful activity. The Deep Cyber Threat Situational Awareness System (DCTSAF) (Vinayakumar, Soman, Poornachandran, & Menon, 2019) is the name of the highly scalable system that is presented. To estimate the likelihood that the domain name or URL is malicious, feed-forward networks with non-linear activation functions are used after deep learning layers extract features from character-level embedding. Every experiment is conducted using a 0.001 learning rate across 1,000 epochs. In every test instance, the deep learning techniques outperformed the conventional machine learning classifiers.

Three distinct cyber security use cases—android malware categorization, incident detection, and fraud detection—are addressed by the study (HB, Poornachandran, & KP, 2018) using DNNs. Each use case's data set includes actual, well-known examples of both benign and malevolent activity. By carrying out several rounds of tests for network architectures and parameters, the effective network architecture for DNN is selected. TensorFlow and Keras are used as the software framework in this study. All of the units in the hidden layer's input and output are fully linked. The backpropagation process is used to train the DNN network. The fully connected layers, batch normalization layers, and dropout layers make up the suggested deep neural network.

The proposed process (Spegni, et al., 2022) is the first modeling of precision cybersecurity. It entails seeing patients receive telerehabilitation treatments from a distance. Wearing a smartwatch allows each patient to get their physiological signs. Every day, the patient has to complete rehabilitation exercises, watch films on a computer application, and attempt to replicate the suggested workouts. Physicians have access to certain performance indices that are derived from raw data as well as raw data itself. When certain crucial circumstances are met, the system is capable of issuing alarms.

4.6 Future Scope

Given the speed at which technology is developing and the always-shifting threat landscape, forecasting the future of cybersecurity is difficult. Still, several themes and areas of interest will probably influence cybersecurity going forward:

- **Machine learning (ML) and artificial intelligence (AI):**
  - **Automation of Cybersecurity:** AI and ML will be crucial in automating threat identification and response. Large volumes of data may be analyzed in real time

by these technologies, which makes it easier for security systems to detect dangers and take appropriate action.

- **Model of Zero Trust Security:**
  - o **Constant Authentication**: The Zero Trust paradigm, which operates under the premise that there is no trust in the network's external parties, will gain traction. The implementation of continuous authentication techniques, such as biometrics and behavioral analysis, will guarantee the ongoing verification of people and devices.
- **Cloud Protection:**
  - o **Container Security:** Securing containers and microservices will become crucial as businesses shift more and more of their infrastructure to the cloud. Cloud-native security solutions will develop to meet the particular difficulties presented by settings that are dispersed and dynamic.
- **Internet of Things Security:**
  - o **Standardization and Regulation:** As Internet of Things (IoT) devices proliferate, security issues will become more pressing. To protect the security and privacy of connected devices, more work is probably going to go into creating industry standards and laws for IoT security.
- **Post-Quantum Cryptography and Quantum Computing:**
  - o **Getting Ready for Quantum Threats:** Conventional encryption techniques might grow weaker as quantum computers gain strength. Post-quantum cryptography will become more crucial in protecting data from the possible harm that quantum computing may bring.
- **Cybersecurity Expertise and Manpower:**
  - o **Training and Education:** It is anticipated that there will continue to be a scarcity of cybersecurity experts. Training programs will require investments from businesses and educational institutions if they are to produce a workforce with the necessary skills to handle new challenges.

- **Adherence to Regulations:**
  - o **International Data Protection Regulations:** As privacy becomes more and more important, more nations will probably enact and implement strict data protection laws. Companies must abide by these rules to safeguard customer privacy and prevent legal repercussions.
- **Security of the Supply Chain:**
  - o **Third-Party Risk Management:** Our top concern will be keeping the supply chain safe. Firm third-party risk management procedures will be put in place by organizations to guarantee the security of goods and services obtained from outside suppliers.
- **Threat Intelligence and Incident Response:**
  - o **Threat Hunting:** To detect and neutralize risks before they cause a breach, organizations will increasingly engage in proactive threat hunting. Sharing threat data will also spur organizations to work together more closely to fortify their combined defenses.
- **Authentication using Multiple Factors and Biometric Security:**
  - o **Widespread Adoption:** Biometric authentication techniques, such as fingerprint scanning and face recognition, will become increasingly commonplace. The use of multi-factor authentication will always be essential to ensuring safe access.

4.7 Conclusion

In summary, the future of cybersecurity will be defined by the dynamic interaction of new technology, changing threat environments, and a greater emphasis on preventative defenses. Organizations are changing how they identify and address dangers as a result of the integration of automation, machine learning, and artificial intelligence. Robust incident response techniques, continuous authentication, and zero-trust security models are becoming important parts of an all-encompassing cybersecurity posture. The advent of cloud computing, the Internet of Things (IoT), and quantum computing presents benefits as well as difficulties, making proactive and flexible security measures necessary.

To tackle the worldwide scarcity of cybersecurity experts, a concentrated endeavor in instruction and training is necessary. Key areas of attention include supply chain security, compliance with data protection laws, and the broad use of biometric and multi-factor authentication. To manage the changing cybersecurity landscape, people and organizations must share threat data, work together, and make a commitment to remain educated about new risks.

References

Ahuja, V. (1996). *Network and Internet security.* United States: Press Professional, Inc.

AlDaajeh, S., Saleous, H., A. S., Barka, E., Breitinger, F., & Choo, K. K. (2022). The role of national cybersecurity strategies on the improvement of cybersecurity education. *Computers & Security, 119*, 102754.

Ambika, N. (2020). Tackling jamming attacks in IoT. In A. M., S. K., & K. S. (eds), *Tackling jamming attacks in IoT.* (pp. 153-165). Cham: Springer.

Ambika, N. (2021). An Improved Solution to Tackle Cyber Attacks. In A.-T. F., & G. N.(eds.), *Advanced Controllers for Smart Cities* (pp. 15-23). Cham.: Springer.

Carías, J., Arrizabalaga, S., Labaka, L., & Hernantes, J. (2020). Cyber Resilience Progression Model. *Applied Sciences., 10*(21), 7393.

Chatfield, A. T., & Reddick, C. G. (2019). A framework for Internet of Things-enabled smart government: A case of IoT cybersecurity policies and use cases in US federal government. *Government Information Quarterly, 36*(2), 346-357.

Fernández-Caramés, T., & Fraga-Lamas, P. (2020). Teaching and Learning IoT Cybersecurity and Vulnerability Assessment with Shodan through Practical Use Cases. *Sensors, 20*(11), 3048.

Fernández-Caramés, T., & Fraga-Lamas, P. (2020). Use Case Based Blended Teaching of IIoT Cybersecurity in the Industry 4.0 Era. *Applied Sciences, 10*(16), 5607.

Groenendaal, J., & Helsloot, I. (2021). Cyber resilience during the COVID-19 pandemic crisis: A case study. *Journal of contingencies and crisis management, 29*(4), 439-444.

Haddad, S., Dubus, S., Hecker, A., Kanstrén, T., Marquet, B., & Savola, R. (2011). Operational security assurance evaluation in open infrastructures. *6th International Conference on Risks and Security of Internet and Systems (CRiSIS)* (pp. 1-6). Timisoara, Romania: IEEE.

HB, B. G., Poornachandran, P., & KP, S. (2018, dec 9). *Deep-net: Deep neural network for cyber security use cases.* Retrieved from arXiv preprint: https://arxiv.org/abs/1812.03519

Hopkins, S., Kalaimannan, E., & John, C. S. (2020). Cyber resilience using state estimation updates based on cyber attack matrix classification. *IEEE Kansas Power and Energy Conference (KPEC)* (pp. 1-6). Manhattan, KS, USA: IEEE.

Jofre, M., Navarro-Llobet, D., Agulló, R., Puig, J., Gonzalez-Granadillo, G., Mora Zamorano, J., & Romeu, R. (2021). Cybersecurity and Privacy Risk Assessment of Point-of-Care Systems in Healthcare—A Use Case Approach. *Applied Sciences, 11*(15), 6699.

Lee, M., & Lee, J. (2012). The impact of information security failure on customer behaviors: A study on a large-scale hacking incident on the internet. *Information Systems Frontiers, 14*, 375-393.

Ligo, A. K., Kott, A., & Linkov, I. (2021). How to measure cyber-resilience of a system with autonomous agents: Approaches and challenges. *IEEE Engineering Management Review, 49*(2), 89-97.

Lu, X., Qu, Z., Li, Q., & Hui, P. (2015). Privacy information security classification for internet of things based on internet data. *International Journal of Distributed Sensor Networks, 11*(8), 932941.

Onwubiko, C. (2020). Focusing on the recovery aspects of cyber resilience. *International Conference on Cyber Situational Awareness, Data Analytics and Assessment (CyberSA)* (pp. 1-13). Dublin, Ireland: IEEE.

Petrenko, S. (2022). *Cyber resilience.* Boca Raton, Florida, United States: CRC Press.

Spegni, F., Sabatelli, A., Merlo, A., Pepa, L., Spalazzi, L., & Verderame, L. (2022). A Precision Cybersecurity Workflow for Cyber-physical Systems: The IoT Healthcare Use Case. *European Symposium on Research in Computer Security* (pp. 409-426). cham: Springer International Publishing.

Stallings, W. (1995). *Network and internetwork security: principles and practice.* . Hoboken, New Jersey, U.S.: Prentice-Hall, Inc.

van der Kleij, R., & Leukfeldt, R. (2020). Cyber resilient behavior: Integrating human behavioral models and resilience engineering capabilities into cyber security. *AHFE 2019 International Conference on Human Factors in Cybersecurity* (pp. 16-27). Washington DC, USA: Springer International Publishing.

Vegesna, V. V. (2023). Enhancing Cyber Resilience by Integrating AI-Driven Threat Detection and Mitigation Strategies. *Transactions on Latest Trends in Artificial Intelligence, 4*(4).

Vinayakumar, R., Soman, K. P., Poornachandran, P., & Menon, V. K. (2019). *A deep-dive on machine learning for cyber security use cases.* Boca Raton, Florida, United States.: CRC Press.

Vogel, E., Dyka, Z., Klann, D., & Langendörfer, P. (2021). Resilience in the Cyberworld: Definitions, Features and Models. *Future Internet, 13*(11), 293.

Annexure

Confidentiality

Secrecy is fundamental to the complex field of cybersecurity because it protects sensitive data from being accessed or disclosed by unauthorized parties. Maintaining confidentiality is essential in today's digitally linked world to protect people, businesses, and governments from the potentially disastrous effects of data breaches and unauthorized disclosures.

In cybersecurity, confidentiality refers to a broad notion that includes a range of tactics and tools used to protect sensitive data privacy. Maintaining trust, regulatory compliance, and general security all depend on the confidentiality of information, whether it is private company data, personal data, or sensitive government intelligence.

Integrity

Integrity is a fundamental concept in cybersecurity that is necessary to establish confidence and guarantee the dependability of digital data and systems. The idea of integrity is centered on preventing unauthorized changes or corruption while preserving the reliability, consistency, and correctness of data and systems. Data integrity must be maintained if we are to make educated judgments, guard against manipulation, and maintain the general security of people, businesses, and governments as our dependence on digital information expands.

Availability

Availability is a fundamental concept in the ever-changing field of cybersecurity, which focuses on making sure that data, systems, and services are reachable and functional when needed. The availability of digital assets is essential for user happiness, business continuity, and the general operation of people, organizations, and governments. The maintenance of availability becomes essential to reducing interruptions brought on by cyberattacks, natural catastrophes, or technological malfunctions as our dependence on linked systems grows.

Authentication

As technology develops, authentication problems also grow. Keeping up with emerging threats like identity theft, sophisticated phishing attempts, and breaches is a challenge for cybersecurity experts. The advancement of authentication techniques is aided by emerging technologies like biometrics, artificial intelligence, and behavioral analytics. To sum up, authentication is essential to cybersecurity since it provides the framework for safe online communication. In an increasingly linked and changing digital world, building and preserving trust requires a blend of elements, technology, and best practices. Strong authentication protocols are essential for safeguarding against online attacks and guaranteeing the privacy, accuracy, and accessibility of vital data.

Access control

One of the most important ideas in cybersecurity is access control, which is essential to protecting data and digital assets. Regarding cybersecurity, access control pertains to the procedures and guidelines that govern the authorization of users to access particular resources, systems, or information in the digital environment of an enterprise. It is essential to guarantee sensitive information's availability, confidentiality, and integrity. The process of controlling and limiting access to digital resources according to the authorization and identification of people or organizations is known as access control. Its main goals are to keep an organization's network or system safe from illegal access, guard against data breaches, and enforce security standards.

Authorization

A crucial component of cybersecurity is authorization, which is essential for regulating and managing access to digital resources. Authorization, as used in cybersecurity, describes the process of approving or rejecting permits to people or organizations based on their verified identities. This guarantees that users, in line with their roles and responsibilities within an organization, have the proper access privileges to certain systems, applications, or data.

Risk management

Organizations utilize cybersecurity risk management as a strategic strategy to recognize, evaluate, and address possible risks and vulnerabilities in the digital space. With the increasing integration of technology into day-to-day activities, cybersecurity risk management has become increasingly critical. A complete collection of procedures, guidelines, and guidelines are used in cybersecurity risk management to protect digital assets and guarantee the uninterrupted functioning of corporate activities.

Incident response

Within the field of cybersecurity, incident response refers to a methodical and well-coordinated strategy for handling and lessening the effects of security events. An efficient incident response plan is essential for minimizing damage, returning operations to normal, and using the incident as a teaching tool to improve future security procedures. Security incidents can range from malware infections and data breaches to denial-of-service assaults.

Security policies and compliance

An effective cybersecurity strategy is built on security policies and compliance, which give organizations the frameworks, standards, and instructions they need to create and maintain a safe digital environment. Compliance guarantees that security policies are in line with applicable laws, regulations, and industry standards, while security policies provide guidelines and expectations for people, systems, and networks.

* 9 7 8 1 9 2 2 6 1 7 7 4 3 *